Recollections

of

FLEET ADMIRAL CHESTER W. NIMITZ, USN

as given by various officers
who served with him
in the U.S. Navy

U.S. Naval Institute
Annapolis, Maryland

Preface

This volume contains some recollections of the late Fleet Admiral Chester W. Nimitz and were given by the following naval officers who served with him at various times during his active career. Most of them continued as personal friends for the balance of the Admiral's life.

    Rear Admiral Chester Bruton, USN (Retired)
    Rear Admiral J. Wilson Leverton, Jr., USN (Retired)
    Captain Sam P. Moncure, USN (Retired)
    Vice Admiral Lloyd M. Mustin, USN (Retired)
    Rear Admiral Odale D. Waters, Jr., USN (Retired)
    Vice Admiral F.E.M. Whiting, USN (Retired)

These interviews were all conducted by Dr. John T. Mason, Jr., for the special oral history project dealing with the career of Admiral Nimitz and were done under the aegis of the U.S. Naval Institute, Annapolis, Maryland.

Recollections

of

FLEET ADMIRAL CHESTER W. NIMITZ, USN

as given by various officers
who served with him
in the U. S. Navy

U. S. Naval Institute
Annapolis, Maryland

Preface

This volume contains some recollections of the late Fleet Admiral Chester W. Nimitz and were given by the following naval officers who served with him at various times during his active career. Most of them continued as personal friends for the balance of the Admiral's life.

- Rear Admiral Chester Bruton, USN (Retired)
- Rear Admiral J. Wilson Leverton, Jr., USN (Retired)
- Captain Sam P. Moncure, USN (Retired)
- Vice Admiral Lloyd M. Mustin, USN (Retired)
- Rear Admiral Odale D. Waters, Jr., USN (Retired)
- Vice Admiral F. E. M. Whiting, USN (Retired)
- H. Arthur Lamar (one-time Flag Lieutenant)
- Rear Admiral Edwin T. Layton, USN (Ret.)

These interviews were all conducted by John T. Mason, Jr., for the special oral history project dealing with the career of Admiral Nimitz and were done under the aegis of the U. S. Naval Institute, Annapolis, Maryland.

DECLARATION OF TRUST

The undersigned does hereby appoint and designate as his (or her) Trustee herein, the Secretary-Treasurer and Publisher of the United States Naval Institute to perform and discharge the following duties, powers, and privileges in connection with the possession and use of a certain taped interview between the undersigned and the Oral History Department of the United States Naval Institute.

(1) As an <u>Open</u> transcript. It may be read (or the tape audited) by qualified researchers upon presentation of proper credentials as determined by the Trustee.

(2) It is expressly understood that in giving this authorization, I am in no way precluded from placing such restrictions as I may desire upon use of the interview at any time during my lifetime, nor does this authorization in any way affect my rights to the copyright of any literary expressions that may be contained in the interview.

Witness my hand and seal this 5th day of August 1969:

H. Bruton

I hereby accept and consent to the foregoing Declaration of Trust and the powers therein conferred upon me as Trustee:

R. E. Bowker Jr.
Secretary-Treasurer and Publisher

Rear Admiral Chester Bruton
Subject: Admiral Nimitz

by John T. Mason, Jr.
18 June 1969

Mr. Mason: Admiral, it's awfully nice of you to come to us today, and to give us your recollections of Fleet Admiral Nimitz. You served closely with him, I believe, when he was CNO in the Department. Perhaps you knew him before that time. First give me a statement about yourself.

Admiral Bruton: It's a great pleasure to be here this morning, and to participate in this very worthwhile project, which I think is one of the finest things the Naval Institute can do.

Very briefly - I'm just going to tell you about myself only insofar as it relates to Admiral Nimitz, if you don't mind.

Q: All right, Sir. Maybe on another ocassion we'll get you to tell about yourself.

Bruton: Along with many others, as you know, I served under Admiral Nimitz's overall command in the Pacific during World War II.

Q: Two and a half million others.

Bruton: Quite a few of us. My contacts with him, prior to serving as his Administrative Aide were very few. I had met him, and maybe said a word to him, and had him speak to me; but that's all -- prior to 1945.

I had, of course, served in submarines during the war.

Q: So you had a common interest.

Bruton: A common background in that respect. I also had a legal background. I had some education at the Navy's expense, legal education, but I never used it much. As a matter of fact, a month or so before the end of the war with Japan; I received a message out of the clear sky directing me to report on the 16th of August, 1945 - which turned out to be the day the war ended - to be Administrative Aide to Fleet Admiral King.

I had never seen Admiral King, and doubt if he'd ever seen me. This is the way things happen. I did report, the day the war ended. Having had some good advice, I got myself some blue-grey uniforms, which of course I didn't have.

I reported the day the war ended to Admiral King. I served Admiral King for about six months in that capacity. It was a rather difficult period for me, because I felt that for at least three or four months that I was virtually no help to Admiral King, because he knew so much more about my job than I did. My job was handling the official correspondence, handling, in particular, the Joint Chiefs of Staff and the Combined Chiefs of Staff papers of which there were many.

In any event, after three or four months, I thought I was a little value to Admiral King. I served for a total of about six months, when Admiral Nimitz relieved Admiral King. It was early in 1946, January or February.

Q: He was Chief of Naval Operations in December of '45.

Bruton: Then my recollection is wrong, December '45. Admiral Nimitz obviously could have had anybody he wanted for my job. He was gracious enough to keep me.

Q: That was his custom, wasn't it? That was his custom, he did this at Pearl Harbor. He kept Kimmel's staff.

Bruton: I don't know. I stayed with him a year and a half after that; until I went out to be Admiral Fife's Chief of Staff, Submarine Force Atlantic.

I thought that since Admiral Nimitz was new, and I'd had six months experience; maybe I was of a little more assistance to him at the beginning of his term than I was to Admiral King. I don't know.

I have a couple of incidents to relate later on which will indicate to you that in at least one respect, I was very valuable to him. Extremely valuable. I might as well relate this incident now.

Q: All right good.

Bruton: I'd been with Admiral Nimitz, I guess four or five months. His Vice Chief was one of God's real gentlemen - Admiral Ramsey. Admiral Ramsey had palsy. He used to write hand-written notes very laborously to Admiral Nimitz on various matters. They weren't easy to read.

We left my story here - this is just background.

One day Admiral Nimitz called me in, he said, "Bruton you're extremely valuable to me. You don't really know how valuable you are." Of course, I was preening myself. A compliment. Then he went on to say, "You're the only one around here who can read Admiral Ramsey's writing." I took that in the spirit in which it was intended. I thought it was such a good story, that I told Admiral Ramsey's aide, in the spirit of fun. But the word got back to Admiral Ramsey. Within a few days, there was Admiral Ramsey, a very wonderful person, at a stand-up desk with an old Underwood typewriter, pecking out his memorandum with two fingers. So, he stopped writing his memoranda in handwriting to Admiral Nimitz.

Q: And you were done out of a job.

Bruton: I lost my greatest value, I guess, to Admiral Nimitz.
During this period, December '45 and the middle of '47, I was Admiral Nimitz's Administrative Aide. Admiral Gene

Fluckey was his Personal Aide. It so happened that he had a submarine background, so we got along very well. Gene Fluckey and I have been personal friends for many many years.

I've always felt that Admiral Nimitz's tour as CNO was somewhat of a let-down after his war services as Commander-in-Chief of the Pacific. I think that he felt this way too. I don't know. It was a period of transitions, demobilization, and re-orientation of the tremendous war time Navy to a peace time Navy.

Q: But, in it's way, just as important.

Bruton: Just as important. He had to have the job in order to round out his career. He performed it in an admirable manner. It was just as important. Appearing before Congress, and dealing with Secretaries, etc.

Q: He excelled at that kind of thing, didn't he?

Bruton: Oh, indeed, he excelled at almost anything, as far as I know. Particularly in dealing with people.

This was a very difficult period, too, for the Navy. The Unification process was in full swing. Of course, this was resisted by the Navy. And by Admiral Nimitz, too, up to a point. The handwriting was on the wall, it was coming. When the situation reaches this stage, you might as well make the best out of it which you can. This is what I think he did.

Of the people who worked for Admiral Nimitz directly those days - first there was a Vice Chief, and then a number of Deputy Chiefs, just as there are today. The one who was most influential was Vice Admiral Forrest Sherman - who is now dead, as you know. He later served as Chief of Naval Operations.

I don't like to get into personalities, but for the record - let me say that during the war, I think that Admiral Lockwood and Admiral Sherman were often at swords points on various matters. You may have heard this before.

After the war, Admiral Lockwood was ordered to the Office of Chief of Naval Operations as Inspector General. Admiral Sherman was there as Op-03. It became very apparent to me that while Admiral Lockwood during the war, because he commanded the submarines, had number one priority on Admiral Nimitz's attention and interest.

After the war, insofar as Sherman was concerned, the situation gradually became reversed. Admiral Lockwood was gradually eased out. I won't say out of his confidence by any means, and he was displaced by Sherman.

Jimmie Fife was on the side-lines, and he observed this too. He and Sherman didn't get along too well either - for the record. Fife was smart enough and able enough to handle this situation quite well. I think that as far as personal affection was concerned, Admiral Nimitz was closer to Admiral Fife than maybe any Flag Officer that I know.

Insofar as official matters were concerned, he relied very heavily on Admiral Sherman. Sherman was the type of person who sought responsibility. He made mistakes, but he did so much that Admiral Nimitz would continually assign matters to him even beyond his provence as a Deputy Chief. I could see that. It made a difference, it was undoubtedly true.

Q: Tell me a little about the Admiral's relations with Congressional Committees.

Bruton: He was very effective. I went to the Hill with him a few times. Of course, he was an international figure in those days, and was treated very well by the Congressional Committees.

Q: With whom did he deal, principally?

Bruton: Armed Forces Committee, and Appropriations, those committees of the House and Senate. As is the case still today. Of course, Carl Vinson was Chairman then, of the House side. And Senator Russell on the Senate side. Appropriations - I think George Mahon was Chairman then.

On the Senate side I think in was Senator Hayden - he's dead now. I'm not certain of all the facts.

Admiral Nimitz was very well treated by the Committees when he appeared on the Hill because of his prestige. He didn't talk down to them, nor did he talk up to them.

Q: His son tells me that he had tremendous respect for public servants of all kinds, and for elected members of the Congress.

Bruton: There's no question about it.

Q: He also said that he was meticulous in his preparation of any kind of testimony.

Bruton: This is true. He would go over the statements several times and make changes. He was very respectful of the Congress. I again reiterate, this was a difficult period because of this Unification process. Sometimes the testimony would not be adopted by the Congress because the trend was there towards Unification.

My recollection is that Admiral Nimitz did not overfight it - the Unification process. He went along with the Navy concept, but only to a degree. This is only my recollection. It's been too long, more than 20 years. I think he saw it coming.

I might give a few other personal instances. Incidentally,

Bruton - 9

my close relationship with him was only for about a year and a half. When I left in the middle of '47, I only saw him a few times after that. I'll mention a couple of things --

Q: Any and all personal things --

Bruton: Here are some personal matters -- Admiral Nimitz had a habit, he was a great walker. It was his habit to walk home, whenever he possibly could, at the end of each day. They lived at the Naval Observatory. It was several miles from the old Main Navy to the Observatory. What would happen was - whenever he got ready to leave, Fluckey or I would call up Mrs. Nimitz; and she would very frequently meet him half-way. Then they'd walk back together; she liked to walk too. He would do this whenever he could. It was very hard to stop him.

I remember one day in mid-winter when it began to snow about 5:30. He generally left 6 or 6:30, and it was snowing very heavy. He came out of the office at his unual time, with no coat, blue uniform with gloves, and started out the door, to walk home. Fluckey said, "Admiral let me order your car." He grunted or something, and walked out. Gene didn't have his car there, and meanwhile the Admiral's car had been dismissed. We talked it over for about five minutes, and I said, "Look, I'm going to call Mrs. Nimitz." Which I did. I said, "Mrs. Nimitz, the Admiral started walking home in this heavy snow, and

I hope you're not going to go down and meet him." She said, "Of course not in this snow." I said, "I think I'd better go out and pick him up." She said, "You do just that." So, I did, I went out, and I knew the route. I had my car, Fluckey would have done it normally - being his Personal Aide. I caught him, flagged him down, and opened the door and asked the Admiral to get in. I said, "I called Mrs. Nimitz and she said to come pick you up." He got in reluctantly, and I took him home. Meanwhile, he had walked a mile or so. This is something that remains in my memory.

He was very considerate of his staff. As a matter of fact, he invited us any number of times to the Observatory for social occasions and dinner. On at least one occasion, he and Mrs. Nimitz came to our house. It was a modest house over in Arlington. Of course, no servants of any kind; but he and Mrs. Nimitz came to dinner. We had two children then, 11 and 13. The Nimitzs were very gracious. The Admiral would have one or two drinks. I've never seen him to any degree, under the influence. But he was sociable to that degree.

After dinner, he asked if we had a deck of cards. Of course, our children were extremely interested. I think he wore a uniform, these were the days you were still required to wear a uniform. We got out a deck of cards, and he spent a half an hour doing card tricks entertaining our children. He had gnarled fingers, and they were rather stubby; but he was pretty dexterous with these cards. I never knew this before.

I stood there in admiration myself, while he entertained our kids.

Another occasion - when I was transferred to New London, I went up early. He invited my wife, and children to dinner at the Observatory one afternoon. While they were out there, my wife tells me, he spent a great deal of time with my son who was 11; teaching him how to shoot an air pistol. Of course, my son remembers this.

Q: This was one of his great loves; to play with children, and to teach children. He didn't do it without some direction; he always had a teaching element in mind, apparently, when he dealt with the children.

Bruton: Apparently so.

Q: In retirement, out in Berkeley, this is what he did all the time.

Bruton: Is this right? I know only what my wife tells me about him with my son. She tells me also while she was there at another time that they had two enlisted men as house guests, who were formerly on his personal staff - I think at Pearl Harbor. They came down in the morning, after sleeping there, and Mrs. Nimitz treated them cordially just like anybody else.

Admiral Nimitz was very kind and considerate of his staff and his people. Of course, he demanded high performance. But he could be as tough as anybody else when the time came.

Q: I've been told by a number of people, that his technique was usually to establish a kind of an atmosphere; and you're expected to measure up. Without saying too much, this is what he got. People did measure up. Would that be your observation of him?

Bruton: I would ~~like~~ think so. Of course, by the time I worked for him, his reputation was established, and pretty well known. I think this type of atmosphere sort of created itself, since he had the right kind of people around - the people he wanted.

A little bit unlike Admiral King, Admiral Nimitz didn't feel that he had to have all the best people in the Navy working for him. I think he felt that he ought to have his share, but he shouldn't have them all. Now Admiral king -- he took what he wanted, and they had to be the best. I used to have dinner with Admiral King every third night for six months. He lived on the old DAUNTLESS, which was a converted yacht. There were three of us on his personal staff, and we used to take turns having the duty. We never had anything much to do, except have dinner with Admiral King.

Bruton - 13

Q: Tell me a little about that. Did he ever unbend with you at dinner?

Bruton: Yes, I'm about to get around to that. On several occasions - I'm talking about King now - he did unbend completely. I remember one night he spent considerable time showing me his swords and other mementoes; decorations he had received from various nationalities, various countries. Admiral King could be as gracious as anybody in this world, when he wanted to be. Actually, he was not a hard man. Admiral King could be just as loyal to his people as anybody else. Actually, the tough men in my period, when I worked for him - was not King, but was Edwards, the Vice Chief. Edwards was supposed to be much of a softy, but he was a man of iron. Admiral King, would now and then, try to soften some of the personnel actions when somebody had to be relieved. But Edward wouldn't let him.

I remember one time he had Andrew Higgins for lunch. Admiral King had his own mess at the Pentagon. We sat around for two hours, while he and Andy Higgins swapped stories, and reminisced. You couldn't have had a more friendly, and more light-hearted lunch. Although lunch for King, normally, was entirely business. You didn't have any choice whether to come to lunch or not; you were expected to come if you were a member of the mess.

I remember when Admiral Carney reported for duty as Deputy Chief of Logistics. Admiral Carney was trying to lose a little weight, I think then. We told Admiral Carney that Admiral King had invited him to be a member of the mess. You became a member of the mess by invitation. I carried the oral invitation to Admiral Carney to be a member of the mess. Of course, this was for lunch only. Admiral Carney said he appreciated this very much, but he hoped that I would tell Admiral King that he was on a diet, and didn't eat lunch. I reported this to Admiral King, and he said, "That's fine. You go back and tell Admiral Carney to just come up and watch the rest of us eat." So he came, because lunch for King - likely as not, would be a business lunch.

Q: Decision making sort of thing.

Bruton: One of my jobs was to remember what happened, and record it. So lunch was not always too pleasant for me.

Q: Certainly not for you.

Bruton: Not for me, but on most occasions it was. King, as I say, has a reputation of being a sun downer and very tough; but actually he was very soft in many respects.

Q: Isn't it unfortunate that only one side of him...

Bruton: Nimitz was the other way. Nimitz was considered kind and considerate, which he was; and I won't say soft, but in personnel actions a little bit more compassionate. And he was, this is true.

On the other hand, King could be this way too; but nobody knew it. King wanted to establish the reputation of being tough, and he did. Maybe this served his purpose.

Q: I suppose a wartime figure has to be tough.

Bruton: He and Nimitz, although they're opposites in many respects, got along wonderfully well. He had great respect for Admiral Nimitz, and vice versa. As far as King was concerned, no one but Nimitz could be allowed to be his successor as CNO.

Q: Did you experience any of Admiral Nimitz's wonderful stories? He was a superb story-teller.

Bruton: He was indeed, and so was King. I don't have a good mind to remember those stories. I think Gene Fluckey would remember them better than I. Admiral Nimitz was a fine story-teller. They were always good stories; at the worst, only slightly off-color. He wasn't adverse to a little of that.

I remember one day when he came in the office, we had some of the early air-conditioning machines in the outer office; two great big things, very inefficient. When they ran a lot, some of the insulation began to get hot and they began to stink. He was coming in the office one day, and said, "Let's open some windows. This place smells like a zoo." Which it did. He liked fresh air.

After 1947, I saw Admiral Nimitz only infrequently - maybe two or three times.

Q: Where, at social gatherings?

Bruton: No, not at social gatherings. I think one time after that; we came out to his house at a large party, many people. Then he retired, as you know. We went our separate ways. We had some correspondence - very little - because I'm not much of a correspondent. Admiral Nimitz would take the time to write it in his own handwriting, and I didn't want to impose this on him.

Q: Yes, I've got some of his letters.

Bruton: Oh, yes, he would write. After a lapse of many years, I retired too. I worked for Collins Radio Company for awhile. In 1964, I became the Secretary-Treasurer and General Manager of an organization called the Armed Forces Relief and Benefit Association. This is the oldest and largest

Bruton - 17

of the voluntary non-profit groups whose primary purpose was to provide low-cost good life insurance to military personnel, particularly active duty personnel. Admiral Nimitz was one of our members. As a Fleet Admiral he was still on active duty, and so was eligible to be a member. And so was MacArthur. During my period, we paid a death benefit to General MacArthur's son. It was my privilege to pay Mrs. Nimitz later on. I received a very gracious note from her. It was $15,000, and you know the Nimitz's were not rich.

One thing did happen after I had been on the job with this Association only a few months - I got a little note from Admiral Nimitz, who for some reason choøse to pay his insurance contribution quarterly by check. We encouraged people to pay by government allotment; the cost was exactly the same. 95% of the members did. (We had 60,000 members.) Admiral Nimitz, and some other people - a few others, choøse to pay it by check. This was bad for an active duty person who was being transferred time to time. If you failed to pay your contribution, you had 30 days period of grace; at the end of that time, your insurance coverage ended. Admiral Nimitz, of course, was retired then, or effectively retired. And was in a fixed location. I think maybe his attitude goes back to some of the early days in the allotment system, when the allotment system wasn't perfect (and still isn't). Admiral Nimitz along with one of a very small group who chose to pay this insurance contribution by personal check, which he had to do every three months. We would send him a notice. One day, I got a very short note from him. It said, "Dear Bruton, why don't you do something about an abbreviation for the name of our association? There's not room enough to write it on the check." So, I did. We made arrangement with the bank, on the basis of his suggestion; even at his advanced age. It showed his continued interest in improvement, and how sharp his mind was. This was not long before he died. Here he was making a suggestion, and a very useful suggestion. We made arrangements with the bank. I was able to tell him, as well as the other members who paid by check, that they could use the abbreviation AFR&BA. That was my last communication with Admiral Nimitz.

As I said, later on we paid the death benefit to Mrs. Nimitz. I think she needed it, and it was very useful to her. I did not go to his funeral, but Fluckey did. It was held, as you know, on the West Coast. I thought it would be held back here. But that is what he wanted.

I suppose that completes such statements I would make in the absence of any questions. Any supplementary information which I might give you I will if I can. As you can see my contact with Admiral Nimitz personally covered a relatively short period of time, but it was a very interesting experience.

I guess I can conclude my remarks in this respect, by stating that in my experiences I have known some very fine people, very fine naval officers. He was the ablest all around naval officer. I guess from all standpoints considered, I think he was the finest man I ever knew.

Some time later on while I was still on active duty, I was assigned to a Department of Defense manpower project. I was the Navy's representative to it. The head of it was David Sarnoff. (Who was, and still is, the Chairman of the Board of RCA.) Believe it or not, there was a great deal of similarity in the way that General Sarnoff - he liked to be called General - approached various problems and the way that Admiral Nimitz did. I couldn't help but --

Q: Be specific about that, how did each of them approach problems?

Bruton: It was a pragmatic approach. They both expected high performance, but they didn't expect perfection. I remember General Sarnoff - of course I'm getting on another personality --

Q: That's all right. That's a correlation.

Bruton: I talked to General Sarnoff one time about one of his division managers at RCA. (Incidentally, he offered me a job, when I retired, but I went somewhere else.) This particular division of RCA had failed to show a profit for a year financial period. This divisional manager explained it to the President - General Sarnoff. He sighted various reasons, unforseen conditions, acts of God, or whatever else happened; to keep him from making a profit. Dave Sarnoff said, yes, he understood, and he kept him on. At the end of the next year, he didn't make a profit, and he came back with a similar story. "You know," he said, "I had to get a new divisional manager." He wasn't being vindictive about it. He didn't dislike the man, and maybe all these things did happen. Nevertheless, RCA was a profit-making organiztion. They have to make a change in line with the objectives of the corporation.

I think that Admiral Nimitz took this approach too, with individuals sometimes. He would give a subordinate amply opportunity to demonstrate a performance in the Navy; and when the subordinate couldn't, whatever the reason, he had to make a change.

Q: His son told me, I guess others have told you the same thing -- that he made it very clear to his family that his first duty and obligation and love was the Navy. And that all other things came after that. Would you make that assessment, also?

Bruton: I would think so. This philosophy, this attitude is not unique to Admiral Nimitz. Many successful naval officers had this attitude with an even greater degree. Admiral Nimitz didn't neglect his family, by any means. I think he had the idea that the Navy came first.

I know of two people whose names we have already mentioned whose attitude was much stronger. One of them is King, and the other is Fife. Fife was so navy-oriented that I've heard that this had a great deal to do with his unsuccessful marriage. With Jimmie Fife, the Navy was his whole life. I know of no one who was so devoted to the Navy. I guess King was in that category, possibly to a degress that he was unbalanced, in a way. Now, Nimitz was not unbalanced in any way.

Nimitz was a very balanced man, a very balanced individual.

I have one other thing, which I guess I should mention--to give you an idea of how Admiral Nimitz could be tough, when he needed to be.

This was during the war, the latter part of the war, when the Japs were getting very hard-pressed. There were some Allied P.O.W.'s at Singapore. I think mostly British and Australian. This was at 1944, and they were starving. Arrangements were made by the Allied Governments - they were trying to get some P.O.W. supplies, Red Cross supplies down to these people. Arrangements were made with the Japanese Government through the Swiss, or somebody, to give safe conduct to a ship to take some P.O.W. supplies to Singapore; and back. The Japs were told that if they would do this, carry some P.O.W. supplies; they could stop anywhere they wanted to on the way down and back. The ship would be granted safe conduct. The Japs chose the AWA MARU. This, I believe, was the largest merchant ship they had left at the time.

The story is that they loaded about 75 tons of the P.O.W. supplies on the ship, and all kinds of airplane parts, and everything else in the world. It stopped at Singapore, and did unload the P.O.W. supplies. On the way back, they loaded it with tin and rubber, and headed back to Japan.

This ship was granted safe conduct. All U. S. Forces, including submarines were informed by not one, but several messages. Unfortunately, on the way back, the ship ran into heavy fog. One of our submarines, the QUEENFISH, sank this ship. Couldn't see it, it was a heavy fog. The ship was not blowing fog signals. The story is it did have it's lights on but it didn't make any difference in the heavy fog.

The skipper of the QUEENFISH was Elliot Loughton. He is over here at the Naval Academy Foundation now; a very fine person. He thought this ship was a destroyer. He got a small radar pip, and she was running at 17 or 18 knots. He thought he had to destroy it. As I recall, he fired four torpedoes, and everyone of them hit. The ship went down like a rock. They had a number of bales of rubber on deck, and they floated. Also one ex-NYK steward floated - one survivor. They picked him up. Then they found out what they had done.

They picked up some rubber and brought it in for evidence, and this guy. This created a big hell of a row, I don't know if you remember it or not, in the press.

The State Department was adamant that the Navy had to do something, and the British raised hell; because they feared reprisal, on the part of the Japs, toward the remaining P.O.W.'s they had. In spite of the obvious sympathy and understanding of what this submarine skipper had done, he had to be court martialed, by a general court. The President of the court was Vice Admiral John Hoover. John Brown was one admiral on the court. They had one vice admiral, and four or five rear admirals on the court, and several very senior captains. I was the Defense Counsel, for Elliot Loughton. Of course, all the sympathy was with him - the court, and all the submarine force. As I remember there were about three or four charges, and about ten specifications. Of course, you know the ultimate responsibility of the Commanding Officer.

They had received any number of messages about this ship. She was a little bit out of position, but not much. I guess they had just forgotten about her, in the intensity of the attack. I did everything I could to get an acquittal - for Elliot Loughton. The court was obviously sympathetic towards him. We were allowed to get away with a few things, I think. For one thing, during a recess of the court the trial was

Bruton - 24

held at Guam - we got hold of about a dozen bales of rubber and piled it in the courtroom. So that members of the court in getting back to their seats, had to climb over this stuff. Then, after that, they very properly refused to admit the bales in evidence. Elliot Loughton was convicted of one charge and one specification. He was sentenced to be admonished by the Secretary of the Navy.

Q: That was something.

Bruton: Of course, this got up to Admiral Nimitz who convened the court. His action on it, and the sentence of the court, obviously was written by the staff lawyer. It had a Nimitz touch in it. He really gave the court hell.

Q: He did?

Bruton: Which shows, from the legal standpoint and from the disciplinary standpoint - he could do the job that he had to do. Of course, this had to be done. The court really bent over backwards towards the accused. They did make some mistakes. This was very properly called to their attention by Admiral Nimitz.

I think if the biographer would look up this court

Bruton - 25

martial record, which is in the files of the Judge Advocate General - the defendent was Commander Loughlin, and the name of the Jap ship was AWA MARU -- if he would look up this record and particularly the action of Admiral Nimitz on it = it was only one page - he would be able to see that the Admiral felt, that, as always, however disagreeable, he would do the thing he had to do.

Q: Do you have any recollections of the day of retirement from the office of CNO, as he prepared to step down from this duty?

Bruton: No, I do not. I was not there.

Q: You were not there?

Bruton: I had been detached several months before that. I went to work for Admiral Fife. I'll tell you who should have this recollection very well - Admiral Fluckey. He stayed with him the entire period. He would have this recollection very vividly.

Q: Did you, during the time you were with him, experience the walking episodes and so forth - did you ever get involved with horse shoes?

Bruton - 26

Bruton: No, I don't. I'm not even sure that he had a horseshoe court out at the Observatory.

Q: Yes, he did.

Bruton: I know he did at Pearl Harbor. He was very expert. Fluckey, again, would be able to give you more information on this.

Q: Yes. Up at the Observatory house he even took on Truman, in horseshoes, and Bess.

Bruton: I remember the occasion now - I did see him after I had gone to New London. I talked to him about this United Nations job. He was very interested. I think he spent some months in a great deal of preparation informing himself. He was actually eager about it, eager to do this job. He thought it would be a service to humanity. Very eager to do it, and he was well qualified to do it. He was quite disappointed when it fell through. I don't know whether it was India or Pakistan, or both.

Q: It was Nehru who was the stumbling block.

Bruton: My recollection is that Admiral Nimitz's approach to this problem was, as it would be, very objective. I cannot recall anything that he said which would indicate that he had informed an opinion ahead of time, or that he favored the viewpoint of either Pakistan or India. He was very eager to do this job, and very disappointed that it didn't come off.

INDEX

for an interview

with

REAR ADMIRAL CHESTER BRUTON, U. S. NAVY (RET.)

Armed Forces Relief & Benefit Association, 16-18

Awa Maru, 22

Brown, John, 23

Carney, Admiral Robert A., 14

Congressional Committees, 7-8

Edwards, Admiral Richard Stanislaus, 13

Fife, Admiral James, Jr., 3, 6-7, 21, 25

Fluckey, Admiral Gene, 5, 9-10, 15, 18, 25

Hayden, Senator Carl (Trumbull), 8

Higgins, Andrew, 13

Hoover, Vice Admiral John, 23

King, Admiral Ernest J., 2-3, 12-15, 21

Lockwood, Vice Admiral Charles Andrews, Jr., 6

Loughton, Elliot, 22-24

MacArthur, General Douglas, 17

Mahon, George, 7

Queenfish, 22

Ramsey, Admiral DeWitt Clinton, 4

Russell, Senator Richard Brevard, 7

Sarnoff, David, 19-20

Sherman, Vice Admiral Forrest, 6-7

Unification Process, 5, 8

United Nations, 26-27

Vinson, Carl, 7

DECLARATION OF TRUST

The undersigned does hereby appoint and designate as his (her) Trustee herein, the Secretary-Treasurer and Publisher of the United States Naval Institute to perform and discharge the following duties, powers, and privileges in connection with the possession and use of a certain taped interview between the undersigned and the Oral History Department of the United States Naval Institute.

(1) As an Open transcript it may be read (or the tape audited) by qualified researchers upon presentation of proper credentials as determined by the Trustee. In the case of interviews about the late Fleet Admiral C. W. Nimitz, it is intended that first use of the material shall be made by the biographer of the Fleet Admiral, Professor E. B. Potter, and the Naval Institute is authorized to deal with the material in this fashion.

(2) It is expressly understood that in giving this authorization, I am in no way precluded from placing such restrictions as I may desire upon use of the interview at any time during my lifetime, nor does this authorization in any way affect my rights to the copyright of any literary expressions that may be contained in the interview.

Witness my hand and seal this 4th day of May 1970.

RAdm J. Wilson Leverton, Jr. USN(ret)

I hereby accept and consent to the foregoing Declaration of Trust and the powers therein conferred upon me as Trustee:

Secretary-Treasurer and Publisher

Interview with Rear Admiral J. Wilson Leverton, Jr., USN (Ret.)
in Bethesda, Maryland   August 22, 1969
by John T. Mason, Jr.   Subject: Admiral Nimitz

Q: Admiral, I'm delighted that I caught up with you and that you will tell me about your recollections of the late Fleet Admiral Nimitz. I know from Mrs. Nimitz that he was very, very fond of you and that you and your family had a close relationship with the Nimitz family. Would you tell me, perhaps, first how you -- when you first met him.

Leverton: Well, Admiral Nimitz was just like a father to me. I was an ensign on board his ship -- this was the cruiser Augusta, one of the so-called treaty cruisers.

Q: That was in the early '30s, wasn't it?

Leverton: Admiral Nimitz came to the ship in 1933. He had relieved Admiral Royal Ingersoll, then Captain, of course. Admiral Ingersoll had been on board the ship only a matter of say two or three months. But he had family problems and the ship was due to be deployed as flagship of the Asiatic Fleet. We were on the West Coast then. Admiral Nimitz had been ordered to, but probably hadn't arrived yet, at another cruiser, which was going to be on the West Coast. So the Bureau of Personnel just swapped these two captains' billets and Admiral Nimitz came to us while we were on the West Coast in preparation for our trip to be the flagship of the Asiatic Fleet. I was an ensign on board. I had been on board just two years at this point. Admiral Nimitz was an athlete, as you know. I was one of the young officers and he'd invite me over to play tennis or golf -- well, he played golf once in a while, too . . .

Q: This was when you were out on the China station?

Leverton: This was the whole time I knew him. He didn't play like much golf because he didn't get enough athletics in the time available.

Q: It was too slow.

Leverton: It was too slow for him. But he liked to play tennis. He liked to play big tennis and he liked to play family tennis. So we had a tennis team on the ship and Admiral Nimitz was one of the best. We had Red Whiting who had been a Leech cup player. We had Sam Moncure, who was a very fine athlete and tennis player. And Spike Fahrion. And Courtney Shands. And Herby Coleman. And Rex Charlton -- he was on the staff. Most of these people I just mentioned became admirals. later

Q: Yes, there was something magic about a relationship with Admiral Nimitz, wasn't there?

Leverton: Well, not only that, but somehow that ship either rubbed on us all or it was a magnet and drew us all. Because, in the first place, the captains of Augusta while I was aboard attained seventeen stars. I was on that ship just short of five years and I had Joe Richardson and Royal Ingersoll and Nimitz and Felix Gygax. Now Felix only made two stars but the rest of them really went pretty high.

Q: Well, Nimitz made the extra one for him. It was certainly a happy ship, wasn't it?

Leverton: Oh, it was just wonderful. When I got married, after I came home from China, two years after, we were having every year in Washington usually at the Army-Navy Country Club an Augusta reunion. An Augusta reunion would draw two or three hundred people, officers and their wives who had served in the Augusta during her, at that time, only seven year career. For a while, my bride thought everybody in the Navy had been on the Augusta.

Q: At least everybody who really amounted to something.

Leverton: Absolutely great. Well, right now Eph Holmes, who is the Commander-in-Chief of the Atlantic, was an ensign on the Augusta. And he was a class ahead of me.

Q: And, of course, Waters.

Leverton: Waters and me and oh, the list is endless. These were just the JOs but with the senior ones, they couldn't have won the war without the Augusta admirals.

Q: Well, tell me about Nimitz as captain of the ship.

Leverton: Well, Nimitz was a great captain. The crew loved him. He used to wear -- of course, in those days there were no khakis, we wore either whites or we wore blues. And with his whites, Admiral Nimitz had a pair of cushion-soled shoes and he could walk around ship without making a sound, so he was called flannel foot by the bluejackets. He didn't have small feet either. We had a marvelous cruise out in the Orient. We seldom spent the night at sea unless we were going somewhere exotic. We followed the weather up and down the China coast and every winter we'd make a trip all the way down across the Equator somewhere.

Q: What was your main mission?

Leverton: These cruises were showing the flag. Our Asiatic Fleet in those days wasn't like the Seventh Fleet is now. The Asiatic Fleet was the cruiser, a squadron of destroyers, a squadron of submarines, and a few auxiliaries and a few old gun-boats up the rivers. We were showing the flag and, of course, in those days there were a lot of treaty ports in China and in spite of the fact that it was a small fleet, our Admiral was a four-star admiral because the British and the Americans used to exchange -- take turns having the senior admiral on the station. While we were out there it was Admiral Upham and he was the senior-most admiral.

Q: There were a lot of courtesy calls then.

Leverton: One of the main things. I bet I wore my frock coat and fore and aft hat-- well, I don't think I ever wore it anywhere else except on the China station, giving honors to dignitaries. We'd go to some places that our book of protocol didn't have anything on -- a sheik of a little place and this fellow had never had any shoes on but we had to give him a gun salute just the same and hoist the flag. Speaking of giving protocol, the only time I ever saw Admiral Nimitz, then a Captain, really mad, really angry, boiling over -- we came to Tokyo Bay and we were sent up there especially because old Admiral Togo had died. Have you heard this story? ~~Admiral Togo had died.~~ I mean having interviewed people about Admiral Nimitz, I don't know how you missed it. Admiral Togo had died and of course he was _the_ Japanese hero outside of the royalty. So there was a big state funeral and every nation which had a ship in Asiatic waters sent representatives to this state funeral. So there were Italians and French and Chinese and English and everybody, including us. And we came in there in the <u>Augusta</u>. Of course, as you know, when you come into port, you fire a salute to the port. So we come charging in there among ships of all nations and as the first gun of the salute sounds, you break at the fore the flag of this host nation, Japan. So we broke at the fore and started the salute and so we looked up there and, my God, it's the Chinese flag! So we finished this damn salute and hauled up the right flag and fired another one. Of course, all these other navies had seen this happen. And not only that, but of course the Chinese and the Japanese weren't in very good friendship, anyhow.

Q: No, indeed they weren't.

Leverton: Oh murder! Well, Admiral Upham and Captain Nimitz had to get on their best bib and tucker and go over to apologize to the Japanese admiral, the Japanese everybody that they could talk to -- they had to apologize to. When he came back, he was still mad.

Q: But he hadn't had time to do anything about it before he went to . . .

Leverton: "Who was the officer of the deck?" I don't know if you want me to tell you or not.

Q: Certainly.

Leverton: Well, it was a fellow named Stuart McAfee. J. Stuart McAfee. This was in 1934 so we were JGs at the time, I guess. They got the signalman that broke the flag and the officer of the deck who was there. Of course, the poor suckers -- the dern flag had stenciled right on it Japanese ensign and it had been a mistake at the factory. Anyhow, they hadn't checked it. He said, "If I wasn't so mad, I'd kill you both right now. But what I'm going to do is send both of you off my bridge and if I ever catch you up here again, I'll kill you." Stuart McAfee went into the Supply Corps after that. No, he really went into the Supply Corps because his eyes were below normal for a line officer that he had the application in and he said "It's a good thing because I think Admiral Nimitz would have thrown me overboard." Boy, he was mad. Because it was, you know, done and it was helpless to repair. All you could do was go over and grovel a little.

Q: Did you go to the funeral?

Leverton: Oh yea. We picked a platoon and all the other nations did the same thing, marked a big platoon. I didn't go to the funeral myself. We picked the twenty-five tallest sailors we had and the tallest young officer, who was Bill Wylie [Wiley crossed out] and who is an admiral now, too. He's the Commandant of the First Naval District. And marched them down. We wanted the tallest people to tower over these Orientals and they marched in that funeral.

Q: Admiral Nimitz did tell me about this funeral himself. But, of course he didn't tell me about the flag.

Leverton: Oh boy! I'll never forget that. When they break the flag, we all look up there and see that it unfurls and flies nice. Boy!

Q: There was no rising sun. Tell me about some of the other things in port on the China coast.

Leverton: Well, we were talking about tennis, did Sam Moncure tell you about the way the Admiral put it over on him one time?

Q: I don't think so.

Leverton: Well, I say, the Admiral would like to play tennis with all the people and those that gave him a good game, so much the better. So one time . . .

Q: Was he at all selective? Did he know something about your game before he invited you?

Leverton: Oh sure. We had a team and there were ten or twelve of us on it that played adequately. But Sam was among the best. So he played the Admiral and beat him. That didn't set too good, he thought he could beat him. So the Admiral waited his time and we had a big party one night and everybody stayed up late, howling blue murder, and we went on back to the ship. The next morning at seven o'clock there was a signal over there for Sam to come over and play Captain Nimitz. The Captain was living ashore with his family while we were in port; in Manila this was.

Q: He hadn't been a part of this party.

Leverton: Oh yes, but he went home at a reasonable hour, not like the JOs, they had to stay up and make sure the bar got closed. Anyhow, he got him over there at eight o'clock on a Sunday morning and really tromped him in the dirt.

Q: Vengeance is mine.

Leverton: Yes, absolutely. Another tennis story. I was his aide in Washington for a year. When we would play tennis in the afternoon, we'd leave from the old Navy Building down there on

Constitution Avenue and go to the Army-Navy Club and play tennis after work during the summer a couple of times a week. So one day he said, "Mrs. Nimitz is going to meet us over there. Why don't you get Helen to come over." This was in the morning. "And we'll have a game of tennis and a cocktail and then we'll have a family dinner over there." So I called Helen and Helen had never played tennis with the Admiral, or anybody else hardly. So she went over there in the early afternoon and took a tennis lesson, got herself all worn out and couldn't hit the ball anyhow. She was so tired by the time we got there at five o'clock that she couldn't make a foul tip. Mrs. Nimitz said, "Helen, I think your game is off a little bit today. Why don't we sit over here and watch them play."

Q: Did you ever tell her the truth?

Leverton: Oh yes. Another thing about Mrs. Nimitz -- as I say I was his aide then and we would go to all the football games, especially the Army-Navy Game and we'd sit in the Chief of Personnel's box. Helen was kind of "in a family way."

Mrs. Leverton: I was.

Leverton: Yes, not me. Mrs. Nimitz had to give her a lot of help. When our babies were born, Mrs. Nimitz knew about when and she had knitted a beautiful little sweater.

Q: But only one.

Leverton: Only one. So the next day she had another one. She sat down and knitted it that day.

Q: That bespeaks her character. She's not that about to be outdone.

Leverton: Yes. We jump a whole generation, after he retired, we were talking at the table a while ago about the Admiral coming back to Washington once in a while. He came back for a couple of hearings at the Capitol and, of course, he had to come back for two or three of these dern funerals which he hated to do, they were so depressing. Because he had seen his old friends going.

Q: This was at Arlington.

Leverton: Yes. One time they came back for a funeral and Catherine and Junior Lay were living over in Arlington. So the Admiral stayed with them. They (BuPers) sent this young officer to be his aide and personal to go to the funeral and everything. The funeral was going to be way up in the National Cathedral. The aide got over there. What was he going to do?

Mrs. Leverton: He was going to help the Admiral dress and he turned around the other way.

Leverton: Yes, he was going to help the Admiral dress but they had been somewhere else, you see, and he had his gear there and he was going to change but he didn't even know how to put the buttons in his uniform. The Admiral and Catherine were getting this dern kid dressed so he could get to the funeral on time. And then they were almost late because the driver didn't know how to get out of there and get over to the . . .

Mrs. Leverton: He groveled along. He was too young.

Leverton: So next time he came, I guess I was a Captain then. I had them assign me as his aide.

Q: You knew a little more about it.

Leverton: I knew him too.

Mrs. Leverton: He didn't want to be aided.

Leverton: No, he didn't want to be aided. But this aide he would have to aid. So when we would go over to the Capitol for

Leverton - 13

these hearings -- this was in 1958 -- this business about unification and setting up the Pentagon and everything.

Q: Tell me about the Admiral and the Congressional committee. How did he conduct himself.

Leverton: Oh, very fine. Of course, there were two sets of hearings. One about that and one by the preparedness subcommittee of the Armed Services Committee, which Lyndon Johnson was the chairman of. He was majority leader then. They got in there talking about preparedness and so on but mostly it was for publicity for the committee. They were trying to get something over and I can't recall what it was now or why. But I think it was just one of those things that happened ten years after the war like it is now. The military was being pushed around a little bit. But he wouldn't let them push him around. But Lyndon Johnson's technique was to give maybe a paragraph quote and say, "Do you agree with that?" The Admiral said, "Can I see that in writing?" "No." He read it again. "Well, read it one more time." Well, the Admiral said, "I agree with it if it doesn't mean so and so." Because you know it is quite complicated and ambiguous language and Johnson would have to admit that it didn't mean that, so he would agree with him. But he didn't want to get in current squabbles and he didn't think it was right for either him or MacArthur and all the other people who were over the hill so far as a career in the military was concerned to get in the act about what should be done in reorganizing the Pentagon.

Q: He felt this was up to the younger generation.

Leverton; He'd say you're not au courant, you're not in the thick of it and you don't know whether it's better to have six under-secretaries or only four. If it had been the way it was when you were there, why then . . . but it's not. They're not doing the same things any more. If you'd ask me now, what would you do about -- I don't know -- the Pueblo or something. Well, I'd say if it was me I would have done so and so if it had been back there where I had control. Now /I don't know. I don't know what the captain of the Pueblo's orders were. All /I know is that nobody's taking my ship away from me. Not while I'm standing up.

Q: Tell me about the Admiral and Vinson.

Leverton: Oh, they were great friends, great friends. As a matter of fact, you see even way back in 1939, he used to consult with him.

Q: Consult with Carl Vinson.

Leverton: Yes. Well, in the first place, the old gentleman, Vinson, knew what could be done and he really rallied around on that thing in 1958 and got the best deal out of it he could. But there was going to be a bill and there was no way to stop it. With the influence of Eisenhower on the other side, why Vinson had to make the best deal he could. Admiral Nimitz, when he would come to town, always made a point of seeing him or calling him up. It just so happened that Carl Vinson and Helen's father went to the same prep school together. Dr. Bell used to say if it hadn't been for him, why Carl Vinson would never have passed algebra. As a matter of fact, in that personnel business of course, he had a lot Congressmen whom he knew very well. Of course, there's a different generation from those right now.

Q: Yes. But he was very deft at that kind of thing.

Leverton: Absolutely. They liked him. He didn't try to be "clever" or talk obliquely. They trusted him.

Q: In public situations, wasn't he?

Leverton: Yes, without making any effort to be a public relations type. It's just because of the fact that he is a nice and honest man, it just becomes evident as soon as you start talking to him. I never heard of anybody saying they never trusted Nimitz. I've heard that about practically everybody else in the world. In other words, if he said it that's what it is and it's not going to be anything else some other time.

Q: He was a man of honor.

Leverton: Yes, and you almost knew it right away.

Q: Did he cement his relationships with the members of Congress in a social way also?

Leverton: Oh well, those who just turned out to be friends but not just because he's a Congressman. I think he knew all the Texas Congressmen by their first names just because they all were Texans and they're a clan.

Q: What I meant, I suppose, was did he play the social game of Washington?

Leverton: Oh hell, no, no. When I was his aide for fourteen months or something, he never -- of course, I was at every cocktail party he ever gave and I think the only two he gave were for the shop. Now he had some good friends and they would go to dinner together or something like that. But he never . . .

Mrs. Leverton: Small dinner parties.

Leverton: Yes, small dinner parties. Among their best friends were those people whom Mrs. Nimitz knew in the music world and in the art world. They were, you know, some of their closest friends.

Q: Here in Washington?

Leverton: Yes.

Q: She was active then in the art world.

Leverton: Yes.

Mrs. Leverton: Music mostly in those apartment days. They played together. They all could play an instrument.

Leverton: Oh yes, some of the strangest instruments.

Mrs. Leverton: The two daughters lived down the hall.

Leverton: Yes. Like some of those families that says let's play some music and everybody rushed to get their favorite instrument before somebody else got it.

Q: They were a little bit like the Trapp family.

Leverton: Yes.

Mrs. Leverton: But did the Admiral just applaud?

Leverton: No, I don't think he could carry . . . I never even heard him hum a tune.

Mrs. Leverton: He could not play an instrument but everybody else did. Tell him at one of the cocktail receptions you had to play host with Mrs. Nimitz at the door because the Admiral was sick. The two stood at the door, Bill with Mrs. Nimitz, because the Admiral had come down with the flu just the day of the party. So we were standing at the front door looking down the hall and Mrs. Nimitz said to you something about, "Now tell me who is this one and what do they do at the office." Or "Who is this person." And you amused her for about two hours with your anecdotes.

Leverton: Oh, I just forgot it.

Q: Little tidbits about the personnel.

Mrs. Leverton: Katherine Lay brings it up every time we are

talking about old times.

Leverton: A funny thing though -- that old Navy Building, are you familiar with it? How it was laid out in wings? But the Chief of Naval Personnel's office was up on the third floor between two of those wings and there was an old lady named Mrs. Gorman who worked in an office two or three doors down. This old lady walked with a cane -- this was just before her retirement, I guess -- and she'd go hobbling down the hall to the Ladies' Room with a glass in one hand and her cane in the other, I suppose to be washing her teeth too, I don't know. But anyhow this happened exactly at a certain time every day and every once in a while Admiral Nimitz would go down to the Men's Room which was further down the hall. So every morning he would have to stop and talk to Mrs. Gorman because he was out there at the same time. So he'd go down and come back and then maybe an hour later he had to go down and come back again and there was Mrs. Gorman coming back so he'd have to stop and talk to her again. He says, "Doggone, I'll have to change my eating and drinking habits because I just haven't got anything else to talk to Mrs. Gorman about."

I remember one time when I was the aide, Randall Jacobs was the Assistant Chief of Personnel, I mean the Assistant Chief of BuNav they called it in those days, and somebody came up from the Men's Room and said he was Captain Jacobs then wants to see you down at the Men's Room. He wanted to see me down at the Men's Room. So I went down there and he had gotten his pants unzipped and couldn't get them zipped up and he wanted me to go to his house and get another pair of pants. He lived way out in Chevy Chase.

Q: The duties of an aide?

Leverton: I say, when I was an aide there, when our babies were born, the babies were about six weeks old and I got transferred to sea duty and we were going down to Atlanta. Helen was going to fly down with the babies and I was going to drive the car down later. So Admiral Nimitz was seeing us off, seeing her off, with me at the airport. One baby was in a market basket and the other baby was in another little market basket and we've got a picture of Admiral Nimitz and these two little market baskets with the two little babies in them off to the airplane.

Q: I heard about that departure. I think the Moncures were there too.

Leverton: Absolutely. Yes. *Sam and Jane.*

Q: And about the concern of the Admiral for the babies and

whether the bottles were . . .

Mrs. Leverton: He was a darling. Always so good and interested in little children.

Q: Tell me about that.

Leverton: He loved little kids. Well, he wouldn't remember our birthdays but he certainly remembered the kids' birthdays. As a matter of fact, one of our daughters has a birthday the day after his and he'd remember that -- Kim. And I used to make sure we always remembered his birthday. As a matter of fact, when I was in command of the destroyers of the Seventh Fleet -- this was when he was 75 -- and we sent a big telegram, official, through the Western Sea Frontier from the whole Seventh Fleet destroyer Navy for him. And he sent one back to the Destroyer Navy.

MMrs. Leverton: He would write letters to the people he was interested in at the occasion of a birth or a birthday and we treasured those. The Moncures, I noticed, had their child's letter from Admiral Nimitz framed and hanging in her bedroom when she was a sixteen-year-old girl. One of her treasures was a letter from the Admiral.

Q: How did he keep track of all these dates?

Leverton: I don't know.

Q: Did he have a little black book?

Mrs. Leverton: It must have been a big black book.

Leverton: Yes. And it was all in his own hand too.

Q: Yes, he was a prolific letter writer, wasn't he?

Mrs. Leverton: With children in the house/or during a visit, he took time to play with them. He played magic tricks which just fascinated youngsters. He didn't mind if they climbed all over his lap and he would spend time with them instead of hobknobbing with the old folks.

Leverton: Of course, he would make pennies disappear and all that stuff and you know one of his fingers had been chopped off short. He would do all kinds of tricks with that finger. Make it disappear and come back and joined up. It fascinated little kids. He was really the grandfather type. He really was. Of course, you see, he was fifty years old back when I first met him or pretty close to it in '33. Your career was a little bit slower in those days.

Q: Yes, much slower.

Mrs. Leverton: He was forty-nine when he made Rear Admiral.

Leverton: Oh no.

Q: Usually in that time it was in the fifties.

Leverton: Usually you were just about fifty when you got your major command if you got one, just about in the thirtieth year of your career. In those days, you see, you still had to have two chances for selection even if it was after thirty years.

Q: Tell me about Admiral Nimitz and his attitude toward the approaching war. How did he express himself on that?

Leverton: Well, that's when we were back there building up the Navy, you know, by recruitment. We had a goal -- I can't remember the numbers now -- but we had to increase the Navy personnel by about twenty-five per cent and we kept a thermometer of it, how we were going.

Q: In the late thirties.

Mrs. Leverton: '39 or '40.

Leverton: Yes, '39 and '40. We kept the thermometer and we still tried to keep our standards up. A lot of the people whom we recruited then, you see, they became the ensigns a year or two later. We sent them to Officer Candidate School. Because in those days, it was just after the depression. The depression wasn't really over. Work was still hard to get. And we attracted a lot of fine, fine people. And those were the people who we sent to Officer Candidate School and manned the Fleet with.

Q: Did you think in those days that the principal adversary would ultimately be, for our Navy at least, would be Japan?

Leverton: I think that was pretty widely held throughout the service. The Navy had always traditionally figured Germany-wise that the English could handle them, the Navy, but that our big warfare, except for submarine warfare, would be in the Pacific. Well, I was brought up thinking that and it was because of people like Nimitz, I suppose, who brought us up thinking so. And we studied practically the soundings over all the islands in the Pacific Ocean before I had ever seen one of them. Those were the things we studied.

Mrs. Leverton: Did Admiral Nimitz have a great influence before the war on the build-up that came so late.

Leverton: People-wise not ship-wise because he was in the personnel business. But his idea was to get, build-up these people but good ones. I remember one time . . .

Q: But simultaneously he must have been interested in increasing the number of ships.

Leverton: Oh absolutely, but he would be talking about that to Admiral Leahy and Admiral Stark, not when I was there.

Q: And I suppose to Carl Vinson also.

Leverton: Oh yes, but not when I was there. Personnel-wise, of course, the idea was to recruit not only numbers of people but good people. And a lot of people, you see, could see it coming on and those who were going in the service wanted to go into the Navy. It's a better service to be in for the war in prospect. Like my Dad said, you might get in a fight with the enemy but they wouldn't be shooting at you, they were shooting at the ship. In the Army, they were shooting at you.

Q: It's more personal.

Leverton - 26

Leverton: Yes. This boy failed to have his application for enlistment accepted and his mother wrote a very, very hot letter to the Secretary of the Navy -- this was Mr. Edison then, he just died -- who passed it on to the Admiral. "We're a fine and God-fearing American family named Rand (or whatever it is) and some derned foreigner named Nimitz won't let my son in the Navy." The Admiral loved that. There was a similar joke right after the war when Nimitz and Eisenhower and Tooey Spaatz -- he said we beat the Germans and now they're running the military.

Q: What kind of relationship did he have with FDR?

Leverton: Well, FDR -- he got along very fine. FDR liked Navy people and he spoke their language and he trusted them. He liked to run the Navy. He changed a couple of selection board -- and I'm trying to think of the name right now -- but I think it was Gygax who got on and this other fellow got bounced off. That was the gossip in those days.

Q: Was that Bieri [Berry]?

Leverton: I can't remember.

Q: Admiral Bieri [Berry] didn't get promoted at the time that others got promoted for an erroneous report about him from Europe and FDR

Leverton - 27

honored this report.

Leverton: Well, that may be something I've forgotten. Which one it was -- anyhow, I think it was Gygax who got on because the other one was put off. I think he made the Board go back two or three times until they eliminated that name.

Mrs. Leverton: Did Admiral Nimitz have much contact with President Roosevelt?

Leverton: Oh sure, you see in those days with no Joint Chiefs of Staff, why the Service Chiefs dealt with the President and the Secretaries.

Q: It was a closer relationship.

Leverton: Yes. The President got his naval advice from the Navy, not from some political appointee.

Q: Did you go with him ever to the White House?

Leverton: I went over there to sit out there with the newspaper reporters. This happened only maybe four times or something like that.

Mrs. Leverton: In one year.

Leverton: Yes. Now normally, you see, he didn't ask to see the President, the President sent for him. I don't think at all. And this was about personnel matters. You see, if the President wanted to talk about ships, it was Admiral Stark that would go over. But the President was very much interested in who got to be admirals and who got commands of certain ships. So just about slating time, the President wanted to see the slate.

Q: Did Admiral Nimitz have anything to do with the Maritime Commission in terms of personnel?

Leverton: Well, I don't know, but I know he used to talk to Admiral Land a lot. As a matter of fact, they were good friends -- Jerry Land.

Q: Tennis players, I suppose, together.

Leverton: Yes.

Q: What about Secretary Edison?

Leverton: Well, Mr. Edison was a very, very fine man and he made us a dern good Secretary. He was interested in the Navy, too. A funny thing about that -- they named a destroyer after his father, Thomas A. Edison, which was a departure because I don't think they had named one for anyone not in the Navy before and this had started when Mr. Edison was only an Under-secretary. So it was up/to our office and Helen Hess to write the letter to the sponsoring party when the ship was going to be launched. We decided to have Thomas Edison's widow sponsor the ship by breaking the bottle over the bow. So we write the letter. Now, Mrs. Edison had been married to someone else and her name now was Mrs. Hughes, I think the name was. So we were writing the letter to Mrs. So and So Hughes ~~and so and so~~. Now, how to say it because it was going to be signed by Mr. Edison. So Helen Hess said, "It ought to be 'Dear Mother.'" Lawdy knows, it never went out. They wrote "Dear Mrs. Hughes" but I don't know who made the decision to do it that way. I think it was Leland Lovett who was across the hall in the Reserve business. But we didn't have any Protocol Office in those days. Dan Barbee and Leland Lovett were across the hall. They were in charge of the Naval Reserves. Of course, Dan, you know, was seven or eight years senior to Lovett. But those were the two in the same office across the hall, a commander and a lieutenant commander. And when Dan Barbee got to be promoted to captain, he was surprised. Then he got to be a three-star admiral later. I was on his staff in New Guinea. Uncle Dan. He just died.

Q: He just died this year, I guess it was.

Leverton: Yes, not long ago. I saw it in Shipmate. Mr. Edison was a little deaf, as you know, and when we had the funeral for old Mr. Swanson . . .

Q: Claude Swanson.

Leverton: Yes. Now Mr. Edison then was Assistant Secretary. He didn't have any aide for some reason or other. The Assistant Secretary didn't have any. We only had one Assistant Secretary in those days and he didn't have any aide. And this funeral was in the middle of the summer. It was shortly after we came. So I was acting as his aide and we were marching down Pennsylvania Avenue and Constitution Avenue toward Union Station where they were going to ship the body away. Mr. Edison was walking along holding his high silk hat and the sun beaming down. I went up to him and whispered to him, "Just because it's a funeral, there's no reason why you can't wear your hat." Well, he never did hear me and I didn't realize it or he might have worn his hat. In my desk drawer in Admiral Nimitz' office, of course, I was in the outer office with Helen Hess, I had a half a dozen envelopes marked with different names, "In case of death of so and so, open this envelope." These were the press releases, that's what they were. And the first one we opened was Mr. Swanson's.

Leverton - 31

It gave his biography and other information for quick release to the press so they'd have all of that. But that's about as far as we went as a public relations office in those days.

Q: It was really the war that developed this whole area, wasn't it?

Leverton: It became a business, yes. When I was up in the Aleutians, I was Flag Secretary and also Public Relations Officer.

Q: Were you with Admiral Kinkaid?

Leverton: Kinkaid, yes. And he took me down to Australia with him. Kinkaid left and Frank Jack Fletcher came and Frank Jack Fletcher relieved Randall Jacobs, you know -- or was it vice-versa -- no, vice-versa, Jacobs relieved Frank Jack Fletcher as Assistant Chief of Navigation (personnel) office.

Q: Yes.

Leverton: I've forgotten what I was going to say. Oh, while I was on the staff of Admiral Frank Jack Fletcher just after Kinkaid had gone, Nimitz asked BuPers to order me as his aide down there in Pearl. No, that's wrong. It was just after the Battle of Midway, he was changing aides and he asked them to order me as his aide. At the same time, BuPers had just issued the orders to command of this ship. So he told them to cancel the order, he was not going to take a commmand away from anybody. He'd get another aide somewhere else. Oh, I was thinking about the Aleutians . . .

Mrs. Leverton: That would have been the first few months of the war . . .

Leverton: This is in the middle of the war up in the Aleutians and we had just chased the Japanese out. And I was in correspondence -- about every three or four months I'd write to Admiral Nimitz so he could read something besides dispatches and so on and he would write me back a chatty little note. So one time a chatty little note came back and said -- oh, in my letter going down, Admiral Kinkaid said he didn't want to send him a message but just ask him what's in prospect for our area, what are we going to do. I didn't usually put that kind of business and between the lines stuff in my letter. But the letter coming back said, "Tell Kinkaid I'm sending him a package and it will tell him what he's going to do." So they were waiting for this package and it came. It was from Pearl, and so on, and everything and they made me open it. Ozzie [Oswald] Colclough was the chief of staff and I opened it up right on Ozzie's desk, and all of them came up. And I opened it up and it was a cribbage board. So that told him how much action we were going to have up there.

Q: He didn't miss a trick either, did he?

Leverton: He could have written a thousand words in Spanish and it wouldn't have said another thing.

Q: Do you know anything about his reactions during that early part of the war? I mean, some of our failures like the Coral Sea and so forth.

Leverton: I don't know about that one, but just before Midway I was Executive Officer on this DMS and we were going back to the West Coast and I used to go over there whenever we were in port every once in a while around five o'clock and he'd either give me a drink or we'd go out and shoot pistols or play horseshoes or something for twenty minutes. My family had already gone. Anyhow, we were going to take this ship back to the Navy Yard and he said, "Come on in here." -- in the back room. No horseshoes that day. Midway was building up. He showed me how he was going to catch them and we were going to lose some ships but they were going to lose a helluva lot more. They were going to lay the trap for them. After that, I only went back to Pearl

Leverton - 34

for a few days before we went up to the Aleutians and I didn't see him. Of course, the trip back to the West Coast -- where you know he flipped over in the airplane -- I saw him that day. He had just been flipped over and damn near drowned but he was still out having family dinner with his friends.

Q: That was one of his characteristics, his calm approach to things, almost fatalistically.

Leverton: Well, his idea about the war was that we were going to win it, we're going to kill as few people as possible, but you can't make an omelet without breaking eggs, as he said.

Q: That's what he said.

Leverton: Yes.

Q: What about his taking all sorts of personal chances during the war when it wasn't absolutely necessary? I mean, going off and visiting some of these islands in the Pacific that had just been captured.

Leverton: Oh I don't think he considered it taking chances. I think he considered that here was a lull, something that just happened, and the old man had just better get out and let the troops see him once in a while. I think that's the thing. I don't consider he thought it was sightseeing or not. He wanted to maybe see first hand how good was our intelligence about/this place was or something. But I think it was a lull and you knew there was not going to be an action and the build-up for the next one was just beginning. And he thought, now I can take three or four days and go off and let the troops see me and know that I'm around and it's not just a rumor.

Q: He was kind of a natural-born public relations man, wasn't he?

Leverton: Well, he's the kind of a fellow that ships' captains and admirals and stuff would come to see and they'd see him. If there was a conference going on, well, come in and just sit back there, we'll be through with the conference. And you'd listen to a conference on the strategy of taking Okinawa. I sat in the back when we were planning the trap at Midway. And I went back to my captain, of course, I was exec of this ship. He was reading the messages off of the tape and then translated them and wouldn't let anybody else see them. And I told him about what was going on. This was in the middle of the battle. He (Nimitz) thought Spruance was just wonderful. I know he reserved the grave alongside of his for Spruance. Who's going to be on the other side?

Q: Lockwood is there.

Leverton: Lockwood, the submarine man, and Spruance are there.

Q: Yes. And the wives.

Mrs. Leverton: Admiral Spruance's daughter is a nice person to contact if you knew the family.

Q: She's in Newport.

Mrs. Leverton: Is she?

Leverton: I was working for this school up here when Admiral Nimitz died and I bummed a ride on SecNav's airplane over to the funeral. That's the last time I have seen Mrs. Nimitz. Junior Lay wasn't there but everybody else was there.

Q: Admiral Nimitz prided himself on seeing all these officers out in Pearl, didn't he? When they were coming back from a battle or something?

Leverton: Yes. He wanted them to come and see him. I say there's hardly anybody -- a fellow named Joe, a sailor, could go in there and see the Admiral. Nobody got turned away.

Q: He said to me that this had a two-fold purpose. He first learned some intimate details of an engagement that had taken place but he also was able to size up the man if he hadn't known him well. He was able to size him up for some future assignment.

Leverton: A fellow might find himself in charge of something. He's a great story-teller and he always was. He wasn't a joke teller, he was a story teller and the story might be funny but it would have a punch line but still he told it as a story. One time, this was when he was CNO and we were at a family party . . .

Mrs. Leverton: We had them for dinner.

Leverton: Chester, Jr., too. Well, it was at our house but it was a family dinner, Chester and Junior and their two wives and Admiral and Mrs. Nimitz at our house. It isn't often you could flag down all those people at once. But the Admiral started telling stories. I don't know if you have heard him tell it but there's the story about the young doctor and his new medicine satchel . . .

Q: You mean this was the mid-wife.

Leverton: Yes, the mid-wife. Well, that was the story that goes on get me a screw driver, get me a ~~bow hook~~ coat hanger and all that sort of stuff and Chester was sitting there kind of bored and he said, "Dad, you told this story last night." He said, "Yes, I know I did. Now you listen to it for technique." The story is the way you tell the thing. But that was one of his favorite stories.

Q: Yes, the exact word.

Leverton: Yes, that's right. You tell it for technique. I'm a one-liner myself.

Mrs. Leverton: Chester would have been a one-liner, too. He would have told it in a quickie.

Q: Nancy told me that story for the first time and she said that she recalled when she and Chester were there in Berkeley I guess it was and they were standing at the doorway listening to the Admiral tell this story and on that occasion they really did appreciate the technique and the finish and polish that he had.

Leverton: He used to work on a story. "I could make it a little bit better if I said so and so."

Leverton - 39

Q: What about these stories? Did he manufacture them himself or did he acquire them?

Leverton: Well, I think sometimes he acquired them but sometimes another joke gave him an idea for building one up. He used to embarrass Mrs. Nimitz a lot by telling a story, you know, just on the verge of getting a little bit off-color. She wasn't quite sure how he was going to end it. And if he could get something on somebody, he wasn't going to forget it either. He had one of Helen. We were living over in Arlington. This was about 1949 or '50. What would he be doing then? He would still be CNO.

Q: No, he was with the United Nations.

Leverton: No, back in town just temporarily.

Mrs. Leverton: Just back in town temporarily and he called the house early in the morning.

Leverton: Every once in a while he just called up. I don't know what day of the week it was but this was our little -- she would have been three years old then, three and a half -- Kim and she answered the phone. "Who is this?" "This is Kim." "Well, hello Kim, this is Admiral Nimitz." And so on and so forth. "Where's your mommie? Can she come to the phone?" "No." "Well, why can't she come to the phone." "She's on the pottie." He said, "O.K. Tell her I'll call back." Well, he called back and he told her and practically every time he'd see her for a year and a half he'd kid her about it.

Q: Tell me how he took to this semi-retirement because he never officially retired. But after his main duties as CNO and so forth were over. How did he take this?

Leverton: Well, he was a little bit burnt that he wasn't re-appointed CNO. That was Truman.

Q: Well, I thought he didn't want it.

Leverton: I think he would like to have been offered it anyhow and I don't think Mr. Truman offered it because Truman didn't want to appoint him in the first place. He wanted to appoint Admiral Edwards, who was a perfectly fine man, but he had no war record. Of course, he was the one who had been there in Washington and Truman knew him. But the other services appointed Eisenhower and Touey Spaatz and so they wouldn't re-appoint him.

Q: Do you know the circumstances of his appointment the first time then?

Leverton - 41

Leverton: Oh no. I think it was public acclamation. No, he didn't confide in me about why or anything but, you see, he wasn't 64 yet and I don't think he wanted to be CNO two more years but he wanted to be asked and he was willing to do it if the President had appointed him because he was the first CNO that had never done four years and that kind of ~~wrangled~~ rankled him -- except somebody who got fired like Louis Denfeld. Of course, Louis Denfeld was later anyhow. So at this point -- they used to appoint them for four years and, as far as I know, Nimitz was the only one appointed for two, which didn't set too well. Not that he ever said anything in public. He just mentioned it to me. I mention it to you but I don't know if Mrs. Nimitz would want that in the book or not. Of course, he was the CNO and bringing the boys home and tear up all the ships and we just were ending all wars, etc., etc.

Q: Which must have violated his thinking.

Leverton: Yes.

Q: The wisdom of that action.

Leverton: Let's see. What were his years as CNO? '46.

Q: '46 to '48.

Leverton: Yes, '46 and '47, those years. Which was not a time of building but a time of tearing down and that's not good for the organization who is trying to deflate and still keep shape.

Q: Like Churchill presiding over the dismemberment of the Empire. I mean, he was presiding over the dismemberment of the Navy.

Leverton: Well, I remember Muddy Waters telling me one time -- let's see, I was on shore duty until '47 and then I went to be the executive officer of the New Jersey -- but those people were in destroyers and when I went to the New Jersey I had 400 people, hardly enough to sweep it every other day. In a division of destroyers tied up in a nest at San Diego, they would try to get up enough qualified people to take one of them to sea once a week. You see, we had nothing but the old pros left.

Mrs. Leverton: When was that celebration of Nimitz Day in Washington? Was that as he came home to be CNO?

Leverton: Yes, when he came home after the war. That was right after the war.

Leverton - 43

Mrs. Leverton: Or was it a summer-time thing?

Leverton: Well, it was in the summer time. I can remember that it was close to his appointment. He had come back to Washington in say about '58 or '59 or '60, I can't remember exactly, probably to one of these funerals or one of these hearings. It was this thing that Lyndon Johnson called for. I remember because he was chewing cough drops while he was talking. He had caught a bad cold and he got real sick from it. And he was supposed to be back from here to San Diego where they were going to name a street for him. He couldn't make it. Mrs. Nimitz went down there. This had been near the end of the year in '58 or maybe early '59. He caught a bad cold and it seemed like that in those years about every time he came to town he caught a bug. He didn't want to come in the first place which made him want to come back even less. So finally, while Mr. Eisenhower was President, he said he wasn't going to make him come back any more. The reason he came back -- and I forget who the last one was -- I think it was probably to Admiral Leahy's funeral. Which one went first, Leahy or Halsey?

Q: I think Leahy did.

Leverton: He came back for Halsey's funeral.

Mrs. Leverton: It was King's and Halsey's, probably.

Q: Well, after he was fairly quiet out in Berkeley and so forth, what was his reaction to that kind of life?

Leverton: Oh I think he liked it very much. He loved the University of California and he liked to do for it. He was very proud of the fact that he was a trustee and he worked hard at it. I remember he told me that the Governor -- it was the governor before Reagan . . .

Q: Governor Brown.

Leverton: Governor Brown. He asked him not to re-appoint him, he was getting old. It took so much hard work the way he did it.

Mrs. Leverton: Did he use that down-town office very much that Navy had.

Leverton: No.

Mrs. Leverton: I remember him speaking of it. He didn't use it much, did he?

Q: Tell me about his application to work, the job. I mean, the way you say the way he worked at being a trustee, which was fairly typical, I think, of his . . .

Leverton: Do you know I think it's typical of most of the people in the military that take a job in civilian life. They work hard at it for some reason or another. They've never worked for any money to amount to anything so they work for something besides money. It's working to get a job done right and if he's a trustee -- he'd say, "A trustee. What the devil does a trustee do?" He signs papers and he's responsible. But he worked. Of course, the trustees at the University are kind of a Board of Directors. He liked that job and he was proud of the things that he did in there. I know he was, he told me more than once. It was just after it got so demanding of his time and he was getting older and he knew it, that he didn't think he ought to be re-appointed. I don't know how long the appointments were for. That Kashmir thing was awfully frustrating for him because he never was able to get his teeth into it.

Mrs. Leverton: They never gaved him a job to do in this part of the thing.

Leverton: Oh he had a job to do but it depended upon other people. There were so many other people and there was no way to get them together and they haven't gotten together yet.

Q: It depended on Nehru in those days, I guess.

Leverton: Yes. Well, you see, those people over there -- their division is religious and they just hate each other just like the Arabs and Israelis do. The Israelis don't necessarily hate them, they kind of look down on them, I suppose. But over there in India they do the same thing. They can't get together because they can't communicate. Their values are different.

Q: Talk about the Admiral and his attitude toward his own position. Most of the other officers upon retiring aligned themselves with business in other to make a little money and he always refused to do this.

Leverton: He didn't think it was dignified. He didn't think it was dignified either for him or for the Navy for somebody being Commander in Chief of the Navy in effect -- although that's the President's job -- to go out and take a lesser job just for money. Besides it kept him on active duty. Now he could resign or retired if he wanted to. Halsey retired and so did General MacArthur.

Q: Well, and General Eisenhower did too.

Leverton: General Eisenhower resigned on again, off again. After he ~~got to be~~ finished being President, he took his commission back. They re-appointed him back where he was. But Nimitz went with the law the way it was and didn't ask for anything different. Then he got real old and Mrs. Nimitz' knee got so bad that they couldn't keep house any more, why they accepted those Government quarters. But that was only maybe a year and a half or two before he died -- no, a little bit longer than that, maybe four years -- I've forgotten. They hadn't moved into them -- oh only a couple of years.

Q: You mean on Treasure Island.

Leverton: Yes.

Mrs. Leverton: In 1960 they were in the Berkeley House when I was able to go there. You never were there.

Leverton: That's right. He didn't want to butt in on the Navy and he wouldn't have lived in Washington even if they didn't love California, that part of California. He wouldn't have lived in Washington anyhow because he didn't want to hang around where he had been the boss and be kind of in the way. He didn't believe in all these retired people who hang around the Nation's capitol. So many of them do. Now this happens to be my home town. I've lived here all my life. But the day after I retired I had to get out of it, I couldn't stand it any more. Not that I don't have a lot of dear friends here. I have many, many friends who have a reason to stay here except they just served here a lot. Many get dug into a community.

Mrs. Leverton: Do you know the story about him dressing up for some occasion and his driver picking him up -- this being the Berkeley House in California -- and on that day he had been in the Navy fifty-five years and the Marine who was such a favorite of his, the driver.

Q: Cozart.

Mrs. Leverton: Cozart said, "Well, Admiral, do you think you'll make it your life's work?"

Q: Are you going to make it a career?

Mrs. Leverton: Yes, then having served fifty-five years in the Navy. It must have been very amusing to him. He did something awfully nice for me when Bill was out in Japan. I flew home for my father's illness and funeral and on my way back to Japan I had let the Nimitzes know I was coming and they insisted that I spend that night with them before the plane left. And he and the driver were out there to meet me, nine o'clock at night, and took me to the Berkeley House and made me feel so at home. They had known my father and thought a lot of my folks too. They made me so comfortable. He took my suitcase upstairs, I remember. I was so worried about a seventy-five year old man doing things like that for me. He brought me that strong special coffee of his the next morning. Then they showed me around the area for the day and took me out for my plane to Japan that afternoon. I felt very pleased that I could see that home set-up.

Leverton: They were always doing something for somebody. You know how they adopted those girls out there more or less and sponsored them.

Q: Which girls are they?

Leverton: Those Hungarian girls.

Mrs. Leverton: Were they orphans or they were in this country or something without families?

Leverton: Yes, just to make something special for them.

Mrs. Leverton: This was after all their own children had flown the coop. They were probably wanting to make a home life for somebody that did not have one.

Leverton: They like to have young people around somehow.

Q: Tell me about the Berkeley House, Mrs. Leverton.

Mrs. Leverton: I remember a charming small garden where she was proud of her Bonzai plants and they loved to sun themselves and sit out there. This terrace steps arrangement held the Bonzai plants.

Q: Was he doing all the work in the garden then?

Mrs. Leverton: Yes, and she did all her housework. As I remember it, they had no help. It was a multi-leveled house, cozy and had a beautiful view, of course, from both the living room area and the upstairs bedroom area. You could see the Bay and the Golden Gate Bridge.

Q: She said his requisite for a house was three bathrooms and the long view.

Mrs. Leverton: Yes. They had the long view there. And off their own bedroom, he had an upstairs screened porch where he lived and where he slept outdoors even in cold weather. He loved that. He thought that was great for your health. They had a wonderful bathroom that had a jacuzzi bath. They introduced me to the joys of this. Apparently it was something he had gotten for Mrs. Nimitz. This was for her knee. They knew after my long trip and the strain of my emotional upset that this was what I need. So they introduced me to the idea of the jacuzzi bath.

Q: Gentle manipulation of the water.

Mrs. Leverton: It stirs up the water. I've seen ads for it in magazines.

Q: I called various medical supply companies to find out about it but I couldn't.

Leverton: Did you hear the bugling story? Maybe Sam Moncure told it to you. When I was a midshipman, I was a bugler. I was a bugler all my life from the Boy Scouts right here in Washington and when I went to the Naval Academy, I was in the bugle corps and then when I got on board ship every once in a while I had bugle calls. I'd let the bugler go to bed early and I'd play tatoo and taps myself. One night while we were in Manila the Nimitz family was off maybe up in the mountains or something but anyhow they weren't there. So the

Admiral was on board -- than Captain. I said, "I'll give the old man a treat. I'll blow tatoo and taps for him here and really let him hear some good ones." And so I sent the bugler to bed early and I got near the passage way and played tatoo and taps and I gave it the full works right on down his passage way so he'd be sure to hear it. So it reverberated all around the bunk heads. After taps, the Marine orderly came down to the Officer of the Deck, who was me, and said, "The Captain requests to know who was the bugler." I said, "You just tell him that the bugler was the Officer of the Deck." So he went back and told him that and I heard no more. But he looked on his schedule there so see who the Officer of the Deck was. The next morning he called me up to his cabin. "You're a fine bugler! I tell you what. The rest of the buglers around here are not so good. I'll give you a month to make them just as good." So, damn it, I had to get all of the buglers -- there were only three or four of them -- together and practice every day. Well, that got to be rather noisy. They began to get me further and further aft and pretty soon we were practicing down in the steering ~~anchor room and~~ engine room. Every day for an hour I'd practice with these darn buglers.

Q: You got yourself a job, didn't you?

Leverton - 53

Leverton: Yes. He had the last word, too. Admiral Upham and the captain, of course, got to be great friends and Admiral Upham was a kind of a story-teller. Did you ever see those poems that Admiral Upham wrote?

Q: No.

Leverton: Well, when I get home, I'll rummage around through my stuff and find some of this stuff. Admiral Nimitz evidently was cleaning out his desk and the duplicates of stuff that he had he would send off to his friends and I have a lot of this stuff. Probably the rest of them are in his files. But he and Admiral Upham were great friends. On the way to Australia -- this was in 1934 going down for the Centenary of New South Wales -- we stopped at Guam. In those days Guam had a naval governor who was a captain in the Navy. So, of course, the governor rates a nineteen-gun salute. Of course, we had an admiral on board who only rated a seventeen-gun salute. It gave Admiral Upham great pleasure to render a nineteen-gun salute to this captain in the Navy. He just had a heck of a good time -- he just enjoyed it no end. I remember going down there in 1934 and the bar in the club at Guam sold whiskey and water for five cents and whiskey and soda for ten cents. Oh, on that trip down to Australia, we tied up -- this was the

Centennary of New South Wales -- and we tied up to the pier at Melbourne. We went to Sydney too. We tied up to the pier at Melbourne along with a couple of ships from England and a couple from Australia and a couple from New Zealand and a couple from India. Now on the Indian ships most of the officers were British naval officers. They were in there for this fleet week celebration sort of a thing. Of course, we had a dry Navy but we had something that these other ships didn't have. We had good coffee and we had endless supply of eggs. So we'd go to all of these parties around in Melbourne and we would stop back to the British ships for a night cap and everybody would come over to our ships for coffee and eggs in the middle of the night.

Q: Early breakfast.

Leverton: Yes. We took a big supply of coffee. We drank six month's supply of coffee alongside that pier in about twelve days. We went up then on the way home, we sailed around the south end of Australia and up to Perth and Freemantle and then we went up to Java on the way home. We were in Tandjungpriok which is the port for Jakarta. They used to call it something else in those days. I can't remember the old name for the capitol. Anyhow it was Dutch.

Q: Batavia.

Leverton: Batavia, yes. I couldn't remember it. We had these factors, these people come down -- the wholesalers -- and we were on black coffee. We sat around the wardroom table and all these fellows would brew up their coffee. This is pure Java coffee. We couldn't stand it. Our coffee is Brazilian coffee and that Java coffee -- even the slightest bit of it -- is so very, very strong and we didn't like it.

Q: Isn't what we know as the mocha Java a mixture of the two?

Leverton: Yes. As a matter of fact, that's an old Navy name for coffee -- Ja-moke. I remember all these experts were going to taste which was the best coffee and it all tasted like shoe leather to us.

Q: Can you think of any other stories?

Leverton: Lots of them will come to me as you go down the road.

Mrs. Leverton: May I tell one more?

Q: Yes, you may indeed.

Mrs. Leverton: This coming home from Japan trip when you had been an admiral for the first time and had an aide in Japan that we were very fond of. Both of us were fond of Jo and Roger Coffee. Roger had never been an aide before but he had enjoyed working for Bill. So in San Francisco when I returned late in '60 we contacted Admiral and Mrs. Nimitz and Jo and Roger Coffee and we stayed at the home of Admiral and Mrs. ~~Cavet~~ Kivette.

Leverton: Which is the big house there.

Q: Right next door.

Mrs. Leverton: Yes, So the Nimitzes still lived in the Berkeley home.

Leverton: ~~Cavet~~ Kivette was the Commander of Western Sea Frontier.

Mrs. Leverton: We were very anxious to take these people out to dinner together and have them know each other and one night in town we wanted to see all of them. So the ~~Cavets~~ Kivettes insisted we stay at their home and they would host a party with the Nimitzes and include our young friends, the Coffees.

Leverton: He was going to school down in Monterey.

Mrs. Leverton: So here was three generations. Bill had been

Admiral Nimitz' first aide and Roger had been Bill's first aide. And the young Coffees had the time of their lives meeting the older couple. They just treasure that night meeting Admiral and Mrs. Nimitz. I remember Jo -- one time when we were by ourselves when we were in the ladies' room or something -- was about to cry. She said, "Oh, this is the most wonderful thing that ever happened to us. We never thought we could meet Admiral Nimitz.

Leverton: It takes someone like Admiral and Mrs. Nimitz to really put a young couple like that at ease. Nobody in the world could do it better.

Q: That was because of that interest in other people.

Leverton: Yes.

Q: That was on Yerbabuena, wasn't it?

Leverton: Yes. I think it was just before Christmas . . .

Mrs. Leverton: They later lived in that same house with the gold elevator.

Q: The Nimitzes lived there.

Leverton - 59.

Leverton: That was the big house with the elevator in it.

Q: And the Commandant lived next door then - Taylor lived next door then.

Mrs. Leverton: This was later.

Leverton: Who was it?

Mrs. Leverton: Jack Taylor.

Leverton: I know, but that wasn't then.

Q: Redman. Wasn't Redman there?

Leverton: Jack Redman - I've forgotten.

Mrs. Leverton: When Kivette Left? We didn't see anybody.

Leverton: I forget who was the Commandant. Was Kivette both of them at one time?

Q: I think he was commandant.

Leverton: He was Western Sea Frontier with three stars.

Mrs. Leverton: He was. He had the joint job, I'm sure.

Q: Jack Taylor had both too.

Leverton: Well, yes. When I was out there to the funeral, Taylor with two stars was Sea Frontier and Clark was the Commandant. It comes and goes.

Mrs. Leverton: I know one thing. If Bill hadn't found a way to get to that funeral, he was going to be the most upset man in the Navy from his long history of friendship.

Q: You said you bummed a ride.

Leverton: Mr. Nitze's airplane.

Mrs. Leverton: He just made the Navy let him go on that plane with the VIPs.

Leverton: Well, Arleigh Burke and Onnie Lattu both bummed a ride, too.

Leverton - 60

Mrs. Leverton: I had called Mrs. [Bliss] Schuman to say how much does it cost to go round trip in one day to California. I wanted Bill to go and I knew Mrs. Nimitz would like to see him there.

Leverton: Oh, they were glad to do it. They had a great big airplane -- Mr. Nitze and Ed Grimm, who at that point was the budget officer.

Mrs. Leverton: The official representatives.

Leverton: And the CNO.

Mrs. Leverton: And they were not personal friends of the family and it helped, I think, for some old-timers to go too.

Leverton: Who was the CNO -- [Dave MacDonald] ~~George Anderson?~~

Q: That would have been '66.

Leverton: It must have been Dave McDonald then. Cokie Ward was on the plane, too. That's who went from here.

Mrs. Leverton: It was a long trip -- they got back at midnight.

Leverton: We were leaving at seven o'clock in the morning and get back at midnight and go out to the West Coast and spend all day and come back. That wasn't too bad.

Q: That funeral, he had made all the plans for, hadn't he?

Leverton: And it was a happy funeral if a funeral can be happy. I mean there wasn't a lot of moaning around. He wasn't a church-goer.

Mrs. Leverton: There was a memorial service here at our cathedral that I took the girls to. I still have copies of that.

Q: Well, thank you, Sir. And thank you, too.

Leverton: He told me one time that people were meant to be parents and they're no dern good unless they are. An officer when we were in BuNav gave a cocktail party -- an office type of cocktail party -- and when we went into the house, he says, "You can tell they've got no children. This house doesn't look lived in."

Mrs. Leverton: Nothing on the table. Nothing out of place.

Leverton: He thought the most important thing that a person did was be a parent. He said that more than once.

Mrs. Leverton: I think it's why his children are such individuals themselves. He made such an effort to allow each one to develop his own personality.

Leverton: I've talked to them all and there was no regimentation among them either. That would pertain to Catherine. Catherine is as sharp-witted and clever and wonderful a person as you will ever meet. Very much like her mother.

Q: I think her mother is great. I really do.

INDEX

for an interview

with

REAR ADMIRAL J. WILSON LEVERTON, JR., U. S. NAVY (RET.)

Aleutians, 32, 34

Army-Navy Country Club, 3, 10

Asiatic Fleet, 4

Augusta, 1-4, 6

Barbee, Dan, 29

Berkeley house, 50-51

Bieri, Admiral Bernhard H., 26

Brown, Governor Pat, 44

Burke, Admiral Arleigh, 59

California, University of, 44

Charlton, Lex, 2

China; stationed at, 2-5

Coffee, Jo and Roger, 56-57

Colclough, Oswald, 32

Coleman, Herbert M., 2

Cozard, George E., 48

Denfeld, Admiral Louis E., 41

Edison, Charles, 26, 28-30

Edison, Thomas A., 29

Edwards, Admiral Richard Stanislaus, 40

Eisenhower, Dwight D., 15, 26, 43, 46-47

Fahrion, Admiral Frank G., 2

Fletcher, Frank Jack, 31

Gorman, Mrs. 19

Grimm, Ed, 60

Guam, 53

Gygax, Felix, 3, 26-27

Halsey, Admiral William Frederick, 43, 46

Hess, Helen, 29-30

Holmes, Ephraim Paul, 3

Ingersoll, Admiral Royal, 2-3

Jacobs, Randall, 19, 31

Japan, 24

Johnson, Lyndon, 13, 43

King, Admiral Ernest J., 44

Kinkaid, Admiral Thomas C., 31-32

Kivette, Admiral and Mrs. Frederick Norman, 56, 58

Land, Admiral Jerry, 28

Lattu, Admiral Onnie, 59

Lay, Catherine (Nimitz), 11, 18, 62

Lay, Junior, 11, 36

Leahy, Admiral William D., 25, 43

Leverton, Helen, 10, 15

Lockwood, Admiral Charles Andrews, Jr., 36

Lovett, Leland, 29

MacArther, General Douglas, 13, 46

MacDonald, Dave, 60

McAfee, J. Stuart, 7

Midway, Battle of, 31-33, 35

Moncure, Samuel P. and Jane, 2, 8-9, 20-21, 51

Naval Academy, 51

New Jersey, 42

Nimitz, Catherine - see Lay

Nimitz, Mrs. Chester W., 10-11, 17-18, 36, 43, 47, 62

Nimitz, Chester Jr., 37-38

Nimitz, Nancy, 38

Nitze, Paul, 59-60

Pueblo, 14

Reagan, Governor Ronald, 44

Redman, John R., 58

Richardson, Admiral J. W., 3

Roosevelt, Franklin D., 26-27

Shands, Courtney, 2

Shipmate, 30

Spaatz, Carl, 26, 40

Spruance, Admiral Raymond Ames, 35-36

Stark, Admiral Harold Raynsford, 25, 28

Stories, 37-38

Swanson, Claude, 30

Taylor. Jack, 58-59

Tennis, 2, 8-10

Togo, Admiral Heihachiro, 5

Truman, Harry, 40

Upham, Admiral F. B., 5-6, 53

Vinson, Carl, 14-15, 25

Ward, Cokie, 60

Waters, Admiral Odale, 4, 42

Whiting, Admiral F. E. M., 2

Wylie, William, 8

DECLARATION OF TRUST

The undersigned does hereby appoint and designate as his (or her) Trustee herein, the Secretary-Treasurer and Publisher of the United States Naval Institute to perform and discharge the following duties, powers, and privileges in connection with the possession and use of a certain taped interview between the undersigned and the Oral History Department of the United States Naval Institute.

(1) As an Open transcript. It may be read (or the tape audited) by qualified researchers upon presentation of proper credentials as determined by the Trustee.

(2) It is expressly understood that in giving this authorization, I am in no way precluded from placing such restrictions as I may desire upon use of the interview at any time during my lifetime, nor does this authorization in any way affect my rights to the copyright of any literary expressions that may be contained in the interview.

Witness my hand and seal this 22nd day of September 1969:

D. P. Moncure

I hereby accept and consent to the foregoing Declaration of Trust and the powers therein conferred upon me as Trustee:

B. E. Bowker Jr.
Secretary-Treasurer and Publisher

Interview with Captain Sam P. Moncure on Admiral C.W. Nimitz
By John T. Mason, Jr.
Date: Wednesday morning, 30 July 1969, in Alexandria, Va.

Q: Captain, it's very generous of you to give me this time today to talk about the late Fleet Admiral Chester Nimitz. I know that you were very fond of him and that you had an opportunity to know him in a personal way. Since we're gathering material for a biography, I'm sure what you tell me will be of very great value to the biographer when he begins his task. Would you tell me, Sir, first how you came to meet Admiral Nimitz.

Capt. M.: Well, the Augusta was the first ship to which I was ordered on graduation from the Naval Academy in July 1932. Captain Nimitz joined the ship during an overhaul period in the Bremerton Navy Yard in September 1933, approximate date - I don't remember the month.

Q: Am I right in thinking this was an emergency assignment on his part?

Capt. M.: My understanding was that Captain Ingersoll, who had relieved Captain Richardson - Joe Richardson - a retired admiral of the fleet, had the Augusta when I reported aboard in July '32. He was relieved approximately nine months later by Captain Ingersoll, who was later Admiral Ingersoll - Royall Ingersoll - and Admiral Ingersoll took the ship - Captain Ingersoll took the ship to Bremerton for the overhaul prior to being sent to China, the China Station, as flagship for the Asiatic Fleet to relieve the Houston. Admiral Ingersoll, to my understanding, had a family problem which would have caused a hardship had he taken the ship to China and been out of the country for two and a half years - or two years. So, for that reason, they selected a quick successor to Admiral Ingersoll, who turned out to be Captain Nimitz.

Q: What a fortunate assignment for a young ensign out from the Academy.

Capt. M.: Well, I will be for ever grateful for the opportunity for having known three such distinguished commanding officers. What a fortunate way to start your naval career. With Richardson first, Ingersoll, and then Nimitz.

Q: Yes. All of them outstanding naval officers.

Capt. M.: They were all admirals and complete successes in their career.

Q: And somewhat different each from the other.

Capt. M.: Different and yet they were all completely human as far as the junior officers were concerned. They made you do your job. They supervised you closely. They credited you when you did a good job, and they told you when you didn't do a good job. And we were all completely loyal and respectful, respected highly these commanding officers and of course we did our job. We worked hard, and that was a very pleasant experience. So, Captain Nimitz was the commanding officer to take this ship to China and we sailed from Bremerton Navy Yard in late October or early November 1933 for Shanghai. We made a nonstop trip. I think it took us 20 days or so, miserable weather up the northern route to Shanghai from Puget Sound, and arrived in Shanghai and relieved the Houston with about a five-day turnover period.

Q: Your purpose was to be a part of the Asiatic Fleet?

Capt. M.: We were to replace the Houston as flagship of the Asiatic Fleet, and at that time Admiral F. B. Upham was the commander of the Asiatic Fleet. So, after the Augusta took over, the staff moved aboard and, as is usually the case, we had an awfully hard time ~~home~~. The staff members kept reminding us of the way it was done on the Houston and the way we should do it, and so forth, and that diminished as time went on, but at first we junior officers wished the Houston had never existed.

Q: Did the Admiral himself interfere?

Capt. M.: The Admiral - no, no, but the officers on the staff who lived in the wardroom and were closely associated with the ship's officers, and who had requirements of services from the ship, were used to having it done the way the Houston had done it for them very efficiently, obviously, and we were an experienced flagship, but we had never had the Asiatic Fleet flag aboard. One of the interesting features is that Houston was the cleanest ship I had ever seen, and my understanding and my knowledge is that they used a lot of Chinese coolie labor to be so clean, and the Augusta caught on very quickly and adopted the same means. So that the double bottoms in our fire rooms, which was a miserable area to clean, were then made spotless and shiny as was the case with the Houston when we relieved her in China in 1933.

Q: Did the Fleet have contingent funds to use for that purpose?

Capt. M.: No, no. Our contingent funds, for instance, for the privilege of collecting the garbage that was put overboard from our ship, the Chinese would furnish coolie labor to scrape steel decks and chip them and to get down into the double bottoms and shine the copper piping that went under the floor plates which, normally, we did not do. But with this labor given us in exchange for collecting our garbage, for old material that we would throw away, the Chinese never threw away a thing, and therefore we benefited by free labor for the exchange of material that they carried away which we were trying to get rid of.

Q: Did we have any qualms about that kind of thing, using men in exchange for stuff we were going to throw away?

Capt. M.: You say "we". I know the sailors who would have to have done the work had the Chinese not volunteered, they certainly had no qualms, and as a junior division officer when my part of the unpleasant part of the cleaning came about and we had ten Chinese to go down there and do it, we were delighted.

Q: How did Captain Nimitz deal with this carry-over from the Houston?

Capt. M.: Well, I'm not sure that he was in on all of our secrets. After all, it was illegal, I'm sure, to have foreign labor aboard and to have the people do this type of work. It was not in accordance with our normal procedure, but I'm sure the junior officers took advantage of it and I'm sure the department heads were aware of it, and it was supervised and not abused, and it certainly improved the hard-to-get-at spaces of the ship. Captain Nimitz wanted his ship to be on a par with the Houston and he told the exec., the exec. told the department heads, the department heads told us, and through various arrangements we soon were up to the standards of the Houston.

Q: What sort of a complement did the Augusta carry at that point?

Capt. M.: We had approximately 650 in ship's company, and then probably 100 staff people aboard. Also, remember, we came straight out of an extensive Navy Yard overhaul during which time a ship always gets torn up badly, and all the nice paint work has dirty, greasy hand prints on it, where piping has been removed and relined and replaced, and we rushed out of the yard at Bremerton with a tug following us to take machinists off if the trials went satisfactorily. Otherwise, we would have had to go back to Bremerton, and so we conducted a semi-post-repair trials going out Puget Sound. We were on a rush basis. We made a 21-day trip to Shanghai in bad weather and our ship was in very poor shape. Normally, after an overhaul you have a period to clean the ship up, and then start operating again, but we started operating during bad weather, which again is a hindrance to keeping the ship clean. So when we arrived at Shanghai, we were not the pride of the Fleet.

Q: Captain, what was the essential work of the Asian...?

Capt. M.: Well, the Asiatic Fleet was out to look after the interests of the American citizens who lived in the Orient. The flagship devoted an awful lot of time to showing the flag. During our cruise in the Asiatic Fleet, we based in Manila for the winters, from normally mid-December until early in March, we based in Manila and did most of our gunnery exercises out of Manila. We could go down to Subic Bay and operate out of Subic Bay and be in the Ocean in ten minutes, where the services were available for firing our guns, antiaircraft guns as well as Surface guns, and methods of photography and recording so that we could evaluate our performances and, incidentally, we had a very good record in competition with the ships back at home, as far as performance of gun crews and so forth. The weather conditions were almost ideal normally, and the firing season was concentrated during that Manila period, except for some small firing up off of Tsingtao in the summer. Summers we based in Tsingtao. We were normally there from mid-June to early September, and Tsingtao was a former German port. It was one of the beautiflly kept Chinese cities and it was a pleasure and a privilege for us to be based there in the summers. It was a bathing resort. Iltus Hook, which was an entrance to Tsingtao Harbor, was a resort area and many of the Americans and Europeans that lived in China came there for the summer, including my sister and her husband who lived in Soochow the year round and also had a cottage at Iltus Hook. And Captain

Nimitz went to their home or to their neighbors' homes on several occasions for suppers or swims or picnics, which was usual in that area.

Q: That was the heyday of the Chinese war lords, wasn't it?

Capt. M.: No, I don't think so. I truthfully - I can't asnwer that. I don't know that. China was quite orderly, the money exchange, when we first went to China we got about $2.50 Chinese for an American dollar. At that time, it was right after the depression, and M_r. Roosevelt devalued the dollar and took us off the gold standard. That adversely affected us because immediately the dollar became less valuable, so to protect us from this ~~inflated~~ *devalued* dollar which bought less foreign currency, they established a Relief Act so that instead of the exchange ashore, which was about $2.50, our money was pegged at $4.25 per U.S. dollar. So on pay day your pay was logged in the pay records as $100 a month as an ensign and that was converted to $425 Chinese dollars. You could draw your money in Chinese dollars or convert that back to U.S. dollars at pay day - the date of pay day - whatever the exchange was, and end up then with $200 or so - U.S. dollars - instead of $100. So that it gave us a pay raise which kept us favorably associated moneywise with the former exchange - before we went off the gold standard.

Q: Very interesting.

Capt. M.: Yes. It got quite complicated and actually on a cruise during the summer and the winter we had a fixed schedule in Tsingtao and Manila, and in between time we'd cruise. One fall we left Tsingtao, stopped at Shanghai, Hong Kong, and then went on to Guam and to Australia, and around Australia and back up to the Dutch East Indies and the Philippines.

Q: On a trip like that, you were accompanied by destroyers?

Capt. M.: No, we were by ourselves.

Q: With the flag on...?

Capt. M.: With the flag on board, yes. Another fall we made a cruise through the Philippine archipelago and went down to Singapore and back up through Java and the Dutch East Indies. We went to Japan usually twice a year, in the fall and the spring, frequently en route to Shanghai from Tsingtao or vice versa. The rest of the time we went in to interesting ports. We went up the Yangtze as far as Nanking, and we went up the China coast to Chinwangtao, where our landing parties were given two weeks' training on the rifle range at the army range out at Tientsin, and that gave us an opportunity to visit Pekin in a leave status, which everyone tried to take advantage of. So, the tour with the Asiatic Fleet was a delightful experience. We saw interesting places, new places. We visited the bigger cities and made lasting friendships.

Q: There were no real pressing problems?

Capt. M.; And no real pressing problems. The situation before we went out there was a little more tense in that I think the war lords were maneuvering then for control. I came home in June 1936, and I believe the situation started deteriorating a year or two thereafter, in that the Japanese started aspiring to control more of the Orient and, actually, I went back to Shanghai as a ship's officer in one of our transports, the Henderson, for two trips in 1940 and, at that time, the Japanese actually were fighting the Chinese in parts of the native Shanghai. They had not come into the International Settlement, at that time.

Q: When you went on trips like that aboard the Augusta, was your route in any way influenced by the desires of our State Department?

Capt. M.: Oh, I'm sure that is so. The Admiral made up the itinerary normally, and I'm sure that Captain Nimitz was consulted in places to visit, and the State Department very definitely had to be contacted before we made any of these visits. A Navy ship does not go in to a foreign port without first being invited by the foreign country, and that was all arranged through the State Department, and I presume we would send a proposed itinerary. If the State Department approved they would get permission or indicate our desired visit to the foreign country who, in turn, would invite us through proper channels. And so we always visited a foreign port as a guest of that country.

Q: And with the Admiral aboard, it meant that you had a lot of social functions, formal occasions?

Capt. M.: Yes. We normally had an official party in each port - an official reception for us, and, in turn, we frequently returned honors with a reception aboard ship or the Admiral would have a dinner party or would entertain people ashore, depending on the circumstances. There was quite a bit of entertaining aboard. In the wardroom by individual officers with people they had met and in the Admiral's mess and the Captain's mess by their guests, and the Captain or the Admiral would have a dinner on the forecastle at infrequent occasions to return such entertainment ashore.

Q: In that day, since the Naval War College and the planners in Washington had always been using Japan and the Japanese Navy as a potential adversary in a war, were you alerted intelligence-wise when you dealt with the Japs?

Capt. M.: Oh, yes, we used to exchange wardroom calls with all the foreign ships when they were in port that we visited, and we used to joke about how secretive the Japanese were. They were very careful to cover enerything when we would go aboard to call or exchange calls with them...

Q: You mean their guns...?

Capt. M.: Their guns and their armaments or other machinery that they did not want us to see, and they would normally take us to their wardroom area or, if they were having a reception aboard ship, everything would be covered with canvas and they would be very insistent that we not wander around the ship. On the other hand, we used to invite the Japanese to walk around on deck on our ship - we were proud of the ship- it was in good shape and we didn't think they were seeing anything they didn't already have complete descriptions of. We felt the Japanese were very intelligence conscious, and were extremely well informed on our operations and on our equipment. The visits to Japan, usually two a year for approximately ten days, where we visited Yokohama and - which is the port to Tokyo - and we used to stop in Kobe regularly. That gave us an opportunity as individuals to visit interesting places as Kyoto and other interesting areas...

Q: You weren't restricted?

Capt. M.: Weren't restricted at all. We felt that sometimes taxis were designated to pick us up and take us home, that was if one of the few drivers who spoke any English and we weren't sure that their purpose wasn't just to listen to our conversation on the wayback to the ship - to and fro. But we played golf with the Japanese. The Japanese had a Japanese-American Club in Tokyo, where most of the graduates from American University belonged, and they had us play golf on at least two occasions. We played tennis frequently with Japanese citizens who were the leaders in the area, who had been to America to college, who were the wealthy Japanese, and frequently had attractive young girls - daughters - who welcomed us to little parties at which the Japanese and Americans were mixed or be mostly Japanese girls with a few brothers and the young officers from the ship. We, unfortunately, most of us, did not learn any Japanese, and the Japanese we met all spoke English, so we were lazy and they spoke our language and we didn't bother to...

Q: It really would have stood you in good stead later on if you had.

Capt. M.: Yes, certainly. Yes, the lack of Japanese language capabilities was a serious drawback in the early parts of the war. During these periods Captain Nimitz frequently invited me to play tennis with him, in that he and I played approximately the same sort of game...

Q: How did he learn that?

Capt. M.: Well, he encouraged the officers to go ashore and play sports in the afternoons. I think probably it was better for us to be on the tennis court at the Army and Navy Club at Manila, instead of in the bar. As our father protector he saw that we got on the tennis court, and the ship had a tennis...

Q: Burned up your energy?

Capt. M.: Yes. The ship had a tennis team and we played other British ships particularly and Japanese ships. We played the Japanese contingent in Tsingtao one summer at a tennis match. We played a lot of tennis in Manila and, I remember, our places on the tennis team were earned by beating your - running a ladder, tennis ladder, and the best man played No. 1 and on down the line. And I remember very distinctly one afternoon in Manila, Captain Nimitz invited me to play singles...

Q: He'd been looking at the record?

Capt. M.: He normally preferred doubles, but he asked me to play singles ahead of time, and we went over to have our match, and in a game the day before, he had stepped in a hole between the courts. They had grass areas between each court, and he had twisted his back a little bit and his back was probably bothering him, but he didn't let that stop our tennis match, and I beat him for the first and only time.

And the next morning at 7.30 his orderly came down and rudely awakened me and said the gig would be alongside at 1.30 and we'd have another tennis match.

Q: A return engagement?

Capt. M.: Return engagem-ent, and the Captain beat me very handily.

Q: Oh, he did?

Capt. M.: Yes. But he was a great competitor. He played as - on the ship's team when we played British ships, he played with us when we played civilians, and then he played with the ship's officers at every opportunity. As a matter of fact, Captain Nimitz and Commander Whiting - later Admiral F. E. M. Whiting, who was our executive officer, used to play Lieutenant Leverton & me quite frequently, and they enjoyed very much whipping us young upstarts. And then when we came back to the United States for duty after our tour in China, Captain Nimitz was Chief of Naval Personnel, present title, then it was called Chief of the Bureau of Navigation, and Leverton was his aide for one year and I was at the Naval Gun Factory as officer in charge of the fire-control school, and Captain Whiting was then on duty in BuPers as head of recruiting. And we frequently went off to the Army and Navy Country Club and played doubles.

Q: The four of you?

Capt. M.: The four of us, and our ladies would meet us at the Club and join us for drinks after tennis, and that went for the two years I was there on duty. The Neutrality Patrol came along about then and I went back to sea from PG school in Annapolis. But the Admiral had told me he would like to have me relieve Leverton as an aide when Leverton finished his one year tour, which was the normal tour at that time. In the meantime, the Neutrality Patrol came along and we all went back to sea on World War I destroyers to perform our duties in the Neutrality Patrol and the aides' jobs all were picked up by Reserve officers. As I remember there was a young Reserve lieutenant named Lamar who went in as the Admiral's aide and went on to the Pacific with him a year or two later. But when I came back to shore duty after one year with the Neutrality Patrol, I was ordered to the Naval Weapons Plant, where - it was called the Naval Gun Factory - the fire-control school had operated, and I spent two years there, then went off on the Alabama in World War II.

Q: Reverting back to the Far East, and Manila, and tennis games, when you played with the Captain like that, was rank obliterated?

Capt. M.: Well, I don't think you could ever say it's obliterated. I think that if you were playing with your father, you always have a certain amount of respect for an older man, and especially one like Captain Nimitz. It was a first-name basis in addressing us, but we never knocked off rates, as we called it, with the senior officers. Although we would try our best to beat them at tennis, and we were informal about it, there never was a complete familiarity and I think...

Q: He was always "Captain"?

Capt. M.: He was always Captain Nimitz and Commander Whiting, never Red or Chester. Now, to their backs, we were a little less formal than to their faces, and that was just general practice, I think. I've never seen it otherwise.

Q: Now, when he was out there on the *Augusta*, the family was out in China, too. Did you see anything of them?

Capt. M.: Yes. We used to call regularly. As junior officers we were told to call on the commanding officer at his home and we would call and leave cards, and the young daughters would chide us a bit about trying to make our number by calling on the captain, and so forth and so on, but the visits were always very pleasant, and we enjoyed Mrs. Nimitz and the two girls who were there at the time.

Q: Who was there, Nancy and...?

Capt. M.: Nancy and Catherine, and Catherine later married James Lay, who was my roommate aboard the *Augusta*.

Q: Oh, he was?

Capt. M.: Yes. Junior Lay, we used to call him. He and Catherine were married, oh, several years after this tour. The Nimitzes came to China and were in Shanghai and I remember they went to Soochow on one or two occasions, where my sister's home was, and, as I remember, my sister and her husband enjoyed very much a visit from the Nimitzes for a day's outing in Soochow.

Q: Was young Chester out there?

Capt. M.: Young Chester was not. He was a Midshipman at the Naval Academy at the time.

Q: I see.

Q: Did you go to the Nimitzes for dinner any time?

Capt. M.: I don't remember doing so in China because they were frequently living in temporary quarters and so forth, but back in the States after the War, we were invited to the Nimitzes - the Levertons were here at that time. The Nimitzes would be included when we were at dinner at the Levertons and we tried to reciprocate by getting them over to our place occasionally. And, years later, when the Admiral was the Chief of Naval Operations, Muddy Waters who was another classmate aboard, and I took our wives to call on the Nimitzes at the CNO's quarters, which was a bit unusual for junior officers to call on the CNO- but we felt that regard for the Nimitz family, and they seemed very happy to have us come and call on them. We regarded the family very highly because they were always friendly and interested in the junior officers, and we felt that the ladies watched our behavior and didn't hesitate to let the word be known if they thought we were kicking over the traces too much or too enthusiastically, so that I think it was a very good restraining influence on a bunch of young officers on the China Station, with money to spend and all the entertainment available you can imagine.

Q: Did you squire any of the Nimitz girls?

Capt. M.: No, not particularly. Truthfully, I think the girls did not have a very gay time because we all felt that if we had dates with the captain's daughters we were polishing the apple, and I think that did more to keep us away from the Nimitzes than anything else.

Q: It didn't keep Junior Lay away.

Capt. M.: Well, after we got back from China. I don't think Junior dated Catherine out in the Philippines. I don't know this, but I think his courtship started when he got back to the States. I don't know that. Actually, we used to gather in groups at the Army and Navy Club in Manila and in Shanghai at the French Club, and if there were one or two girls, six or eight of the officers would join and we'd go dancing together, go to dinner, and have drinks, and nobody courted anyone particularly seriously out on the China Station. We felt that we should wait until we got home before we thought about getting married.

Q: And you couldn't do much on $100 a month, anyway.

Capt. M.: No. Well, it was $125 less 15 per cent. But we made junior lieutenants while our class was out there, and we had our wetting down party at Commander Whiting's home on Iltus Hook, which he had rented from the American Standard Oil representative, and it was a lovely big place and he made it available for 8 or 10 JO's to have their wetting down party, and it was a very gay party.

Q: Do you recall any specific anecdotes about Captain Nimitz out on the Augusta?

Capt. M.: Well, one interesting thing - I have a picture here. This is taken in Shanghai, and that was the day he was relieved of command of Augusta by Captain Gygax, and he and Mrs. Nimitz and the family were coming home on the S.S. President Coolidge, which was moored two buoys upriver from the Augusta. So, after the ceremony in our full-dress uniform, with swords fore and aft. epaulettes, and the works, we rowed him ashore - or to the President Coolidge, which was just a hundred yards upriver from us. Fortunately we rowed him to the Coolidge on a flood tide, we went aboard, tied up the boat, and went aboard to the bar with the Captain, and had a drink, and by that time the tide had shifted and we rowed back to the Augusta on the ebb tide. We scheduled that one very well. And the crew aboard Augusta were quite curious watching the 12 junior officers in full-dress uniform rowing a whale boat.

Q: Did the Captain depart with some regrets?

Capt. M.: Oh, I'm sure he did because the Augusta was a marvelous command. There was a wonderul spirit of camaraderie aboard among the officers and the crew, and that was due, I think, to a great part, to the wonderful leadership we got from Captain Nimitz, to the fact that we were in these isolated ports where the families knew each other and had each other for support, where the junior officers knew the officers' families, and we knew the children by name, and the wives by name. We met them at the clubs, we danced with them at parties. We went to cocktail parties with them when the visiting ships of other navies were in, the families were always included in these receptions, and there was a very close friendship among the families out on the China Station. And we got to know our enlisted crew much better than we do under normal conditions because the ship went to China and nobody left for approximately two years. Everybody had their enlistment to serve before he was sent off to China because in those days there was only surface transportation. So in a division of 60 men, 50 men, you probably didn't have a ten per cent turnover in two years. Nowadays, you have a 50 per cent turnover a year because of the tremendous turnover in the service. And in those days your petty officers were experienced, they were reliable, and they came to you for help, and you went and helped your crew when you could. We had very few married enlisted men in the ship, and they had to be at least a second-class petty officer before their families were allowed to come to China at government expense. For instance, I would venture to say that probably not more than 10 per cent of the crew were married in those days - the enlisted men - and of the 10 per cent who were married, they probably didn't have 5 per cent, or half of them, had their wives in China. The officers on Augusta, for instance, oh, half were married, half were not. Nowadays, 90 per cent are married, and when a ship picks up and goes it causes a problem, but in those days when we were told - in San Pedro Harbor we got a message one day saying that we would relieve the Houston in China, we were elated in the JO areas, and many of our classmates and associates from other ships came over to see if anybody wanted to swap assignments and not go to China. We had in my class one officer who didn't go. He was married and his wife was just about to have a baby, and he thought it was better that he not go and there were dozens of people to swap with him. Another one. Lloyd Muston, [now Vice Adm. Mustin,] who had been married for approximately a year, went to China with us and his wife joined us and we saw a lot of Emily and Lloyd and their one youngster, Henry, out on the China station. Herbie Coleman, another classmate, was married during the stay in Bremerton and his wife met us - Georgeanne - met us in China. Unfortunately, Herbie was killed during World War II in a destroyer, he was the executive office in the USS Barton, and I see Mrs. Coleman, who has remarried a very close friend of Herbie's, Dick Mohan, who is a retired naval captain, and I see them frequently.

Q: Perhaps you'd comment on the fact that if 90 per cent of the men are married now in contrast with only 50 per cent of the officers in that time, is there any difference, notable difference, in the spirit in the dedication to the job as a naval officer?

Capt. M.: Oh, there's no question in my mind that it's a disadvantage to be married as a junior officer, because your primary interests are with your family, which is proper, and they're not with the ship. In our day, as a bachelor, you'd go ashore one time - you had the duty one day in four - go ashore one day in three or maybe two days, and other times if you were broke you stayed aboard, had a nice dinner, went to the movies and got some paper work done. And in an emergency or at unusual times, it was very desriable to have a few extra officers aboard. That is not the case nowadays with more of the people married because they want to go home at every opportunity, which is understandable. So I feel that the Navy was stronger and the people were more dedicated in those days because it was their home. The <u>Augusta</u> was our home for four years. We were delighted to get off on leave. During our stay in Manila, they were very generous about that. They let bachelors go up to Bagio for leave at Christmas time, because we were away from home and Bagio had open fires at night and that sort of thing. It was in the mountains in the Philippines, and five or six or seven of us would go up together and have a very pleasant Christmas vacation. The families stayed in Manila and the married men would help take our duties while we were gone at this time. We would take their duties at other places.

Q: You spoke some time back of Captain Nimitz as being a father figure and I - would you implement that in terms of his own personality?

Capt. M.: Well, Captain Nimitz was a mature individual and considerably older than we were, and we looked upon him as our commanding officer and our best friend. He was always willing to help us if we had a problem. He insisted that we do our jobs, he was a strict taskmaster, but he always was compassionate and understood the difficulties and the problems and was reasonable.

Q: Can you give me an illustration of his compassion?

Capt. M.: Well, this isn't exactly of his compassion. We were going through the Philippine islands where the waters were not charted too accurately, and so he put a couple of us up in the tops of the ship to try to look for coral reefs, and we, of course, didn't know he was on the bridge, and it came time for breakfast. We'd been up there since daylight, so we told the officer of the deck we wanted some relief, we wanted them right away, we were hungry. The Captain got on the voice tube and told us that he would relieve us in due course, but our first interest should be those coral reefs. That was perfectly proper, he was strict about it, but he was aware and he soon had reliefs up for us, whereas the officer of the deck may have had a little more trouble in getting the reliefs up promptly because this was a special assignment and we hadn't prepared for it. I remember another instance when the Captain held mast. It was a great privilege to attend his mast, which is the captain's non-judicial punishment for men who have been reported for infractions of the rules. One of our fire-control men, a second class fire-control man, who was quite a character had been sent ashore on patrol in Tsingtao and he had been caught by the patrol officer in one of the houses where he should not have been. So he was brought to mast, and the Captain said, "Now, young man, what do you have to say?" And he said, "Captain, you've always told me how important it is to keep my uniform in perfect condition at all times and especially when I'm on patrol duty. I had a torn sleeve that I tore getting out of the boat coming on duty, and I knew one of the girls that lived in this house, so I went by and got her to sew up my jacket for me, and that's the reason the patrol officer caught me in her room without my uniform on. She was sewing up my jacket." So Captain Nimitz laughed. He said that was the best story and the quickest thinking he'd ever heard - "case dismissed." Well, there's no question that our fire-control man could have been punished, but he was a good man, he did a good job aboard ship, and a punishment such as this - neglect of duty on shore patrol - would have probably been right severe, and I'm sure our fire-control man did not do such a trick again. On the other hand, we had Captain Puller, who later was General Chesty Puller, USMC aboard as Captain of the Marine guard, and it was interesting when one of his men was brought to mast. I will never forget, I was attending mast - it was the normal procedure for the division officer to come up and say, "Captain, this man, who has been accused of such-and-such has done a good job. He's a reliable man aboard ship. He sometimes gets into trouble ashore, but generally he behaves himself and is a credit to the ship." Well, that's usually the division officer's attitude and I guess it's youth and inexperience, they feel that they've got to say a good word. Sometimes the Captain doesn;t pay too much attention, sometimes, he does. But they had one of Puller's Marine sentries charged with being asleep on watch, and, to our great surprise, including Captain Nimitz' surprise, when he asked Puller if he had any comments, he said, "I certainly do, Captain. Get rid of the SOB. He's not a Marine if he goes to sleep on watch. I never want to see him again." And that was completely contrary to the usual pattern. So Captain Nimitz, I'm sure, gave him a court-martial for sleeping in watch, I've forgotten the details. So he used good judgment. He let a man off occasionally. He gave some strict punishment, occasionally. And he always had that milk of human kindness that tempered his decisions, and that, I think, is one of the things that appealed to us so strongly.

Q: His son told me that one of his characteristics, as he observed it and felt it, was this unspoken expectancy of certain standards that must be maintained, and somehow or other you knew this. You knew what standards he set for himself, as an example, but you knew without having him lecture you. You knew what he expected of you. Did this carry over to the junior officers?

Capt. M.: Well, it certainly did. I never remember the Captain getting everyone together and telling us that we should be doing this or we should be doing that. We knew we were supposed to have high standards and I presume that it was by the Captain's personal example, which was always exemplary. We were aware of his standards and what he expected that of us. I presume that if somebody strayed from the line a bit, the Captain sent for them and privately expressed his displeasure and that his standards were such. Fortunately, I didn't have that sort of a meeting with him. I probably slipped the line occasionally, but maybe I didn't get caught or what, but I never was reprimanded by Captain Nimitz, privately or publicly, and I don't believe many of the junior officers were. The Captain administered justice at mast in a very fine manner. He was strict with infractors and yet he had some leniency when the situation warranted it. His exec. - Commander Hill, Kitchen Hill - was the first exec. and he was transferred to command of Blackhawk, which was a destroyer tender on the China Station, and a Red Whiting -

Commander Whiting - came out as executive officer, and he was a large man, red-headed, and blustery, and he laid the law down in no uncertain terms, and we all respected him but we knew he was going to be on our division, on our part of the ship, early in the morning and we'd better be there too, and if we weren't he sent for us. So that the executive officer aboard Augusta at that time was very much on the job. He demanded that everything was done according to the book, and that's the way it was done, and he personally saw to it. And that's his job, to take care of the details. The captain runs the ship, and the exec. reports to the captain, and I think that that contributed to the happy ship we had. We have an expression in the Navy, a taut ship is a happy ship. The Augusta was a taut ship - everybody did his job or he got fired, and we were a very happy ship, and I think I speak for the enlisted men as well as the officers.

Q: Did you ever see any evidences of the Captain's anger? He was red-headed, too.

Capt. M.: His hair was more white than red when I knew him. Yes, he was impatient with poor performance. Occasionally aviators had a problem in rejoining the ship or something of that sort, which he thought was...

Q: Well, did you have a catapult...?

Capt. M.: Yes, we had two catapults and four planes, and they were always a problem because weather was such a constant concern when you operated airplanes from a cruiser operating independently out in the middle of the China Sea where there were no land bases to go to and that sort of thing. You had to get your planes back, and so the Captain, I'm sure, was concerned on several occasions with the planes, because we didn't have the weather forecasting we have nowadays and they'd get caught in these local squalls through no fault of their own, but then the Captain would be a bit tense with everybody which just reflected his personal concern over the safety of his men and the safety of the planes to get back to the ship. As I recall - I am not sure that we lost any planes during his tenure as Captain of the ship. I remember one plane turned over in landing the Bay of Cebu, but I believe that Captain Nimitz had been relieved at that time. It wasn't in Subic Bay, it was down off of Cebu, in a rather uncharted area where the ship could not get in to help recover the plane.

Q: In the case of losing a plane like that, operationally, was there a board of inquiry or anything?

Capt. M. Yes. It was always thoroughly investigated. The circumstances causing the accident. In this particular case, the pilot made a rough landing and the plane turned over. It was that simple, and it sank. So, was it pilot error, was it unduly rough water or something? That is always determined, and in bright sunlight on the water it's easy to misjudge your distance. There again, if we had boat troubles, boat collisions, drifted ashore, or something of that sort, there would always be an investigation to determine the facts, and then if there was culpable inefficiency or negligence, why somebody was penalized for it. But we didn't have experiences of that sort. We had an efficient ship, a well-run ship, and the accidents were very few and far between. And we did not have the problem of men being injured in automobile accidents and that sort of thing ashore. Well, one thing that brought out the Captain's understanding of human nature: in Shanghai - Shanghai was the gayest port we visited and it was a delightful two-weeks visit.

Q: It's termed the Paris of the East, isn't it?

Capt. M. It certainly was, yes. And we had a great problem. Paris, I mean Shanghai, was one of the few places we permitted our sailors to stay ashore overnight. Under special circumstances, they could stay ashore overnight. We had problems with a lot of the men coming back late from liberty, and they analyzed the situation. They said, well, we're out of phase, we wanted the men back at 7 o'clock. Shanghai just didn't get up at 7 o'clock or at 6 o'clock like we do at home...

Q: After a night of carousing.

Capt. M.: That's right. The city slept, the city just didn't get up, get to an early start like we do at home. So they delayed expiration of liberty to 9 instead of 8, and we went ashore an hour later, and that knocked off the over-leaves. Just that one hour was all they needed for the city to get moving again and get the men away, get them back to the ship on time. Whether that was responsible or not, we, as junior officers, being with our sailors every day, knowing their problems, we thought that that was an excellent decision made by the captain - to send us ashore an hour later and let us come back to the ship an hour later. There again, going ashore at 4 o'clock, which was our standard, there's not much to do in Shanghai as a bachelor, or a lone man, but to go and have a drink, and if you start at 4 you're in trouble that much sooner. If you wait until 5...Then supper was served aboard ship at 5.15, so frequently the sailors would have their supper before they'd go ashore, which was a much better arrangement also. So I thought that that was evidence of real thinking and interest in the welfare of others instead of following the book to the letter.

Q: Admiral Nimitz apparently; his wife understands and the other members of the family, that although he loved them and it was a very close-knit family, that when he was a naval officer this came first. Now this is somewhat in contrast to your remark about the married officers who might have been...

Capt. M.: Now, don't mistake - the married officers weren't given that leeway. Now, when liberty was put back, the married officers came back on time. We'd get one officer...

Q: Oh, no, no, no. I was harking back to your account conversation about the effectiveness and the close-knit relationship of the ship in that time in contrast with the present. But Nimitz was something of an exception in this sense, wasn't he, when his dedication to his vocation came first always?

Capt. M.: Well I think that the dedication of a naval officer back 20 or 30 years ago was stronger than it is today. That's my personal opinion. I think that the Navy - you served aboard ship much more than you do nowadays. The Navy was more a seagoing organization and you were away from home an awful lot. For instance, I went to sea from the Naval Academy and served for four years on the Augusta, two years of the Tucker, a new destroyer that I went to when I came back from China, one year on the Henderson, and came ashore for a matter of two months at the PG school in Annapolis, and then because of the Neutrality Patrol went back to sea for two more years - one more year - in the Neutrality Patrol. So I had 8 years at sea out of my first nine years in the Navy. Then I was ashore for two years, then World War II came along and I went to sea for five more years. So my first 15 years in the navy, 13 of them were spent aboard ship. Now that's very unusual nowadays. Nowadays, you spend half your time ashore and on staff assignments. There's so much - the Navy has so much more going ashore than it used to have. The Navy's repair, and we had navy yards, but that was the extent, and we did not have officers clubs and BOQs and all over the place. We generated our own entertainment. That pushed us closer together. When we were in a strange port, we went to someone's house to have a sociable drink because there was not a club or a naval base or an Army club or something to fall back on. In Manila, that was an exception. The Army had a tremendous post there, but we had a civilian - that is, an army and navy club that was owned privately by members of the armed forces who were on duty out in the Philippines.

Q: Was it not also true that since World War II we are a much more casual people than we were?

Capt. M.: Well, I think so, yes. Of course, in our day, it was very rare that someone resigned from the Navy - a junior officer. But, of course, that was right after the depression, jobs were few and far between, our $125 less the 15 per cent pay cut was better pay than people were getting at home, and actually I remember having come back from China and being on Norfolk we junior officers, I was a junior lieutenant at the time, we were considered - we were very popular with the people - with the ladies in Norfolk because we had money to spend, we could take them dancing, we could take them to the movies, we had a car, and that sort of thing, which our civilian associates were not so well fixed, usually.

Q: Your relationship, as you said before, with the Nimitzes continued here in Washington where you had a greater opportunity, I suppose, to observe the family in the home, going there for dinner and that kind of thing. Would you comment on Mrs. Nimitz?

Capt. M.: Well, you rather surprise me when she - the Nimitz family - the Captain may have said his first obligations were to his ship and I don't dispute that at all but Mrs. Nimitz got her share too. She was very much in evidence, she was a very gay, pleasant person, she liked people, she was so nice to us junior officers and she told Chester, now she wanted to finish her story and he could tell his sea stories later, and there was no idea that he ruled the roost at home. There's no question to that. He was much more the ruler aboard ship than he was in the Nimitz household.

Q: I think she's a great lady myself.

Capt. M.: I feel the same way. And the children used to kind of heckle the old man too occasionally at home. I felt that they didn't stand in the greatest awe and respect and I think they used to enjoy teasing the JOs when they came to make their calls and put on their manners. The girls teased us a little about that, and it was all done in a very friendly and pleasant manner, and they were a great asset to the community of the Augusta people wherever we visited or lived. They had a dog, Freckles, and he always performed. Mrs. Nimitz had him extremely well trained and I remember Freckles even used to play the piano and sing. A spotted cocker spaniel. Mrs. Nimitz could tell you more about Freckles than I can, but Freckles entertained in the Nimitz home in Washington and Bethesda.

Q: The Admiral had a tremendous reputation as a story-teller. Did you experience any of these stories? Can you recall any of them?

Capt. M.: Yes. Well, no I cannot.

Q: Sometimes, they were a little off-color, but that doesn't make any difference.

Capt. M.: Thirty-some years ago, or 40 years ago, I guess, this being 1969 and he left the ship in 35, so that's...

Q: It would have to be a mightly good story to remember it that long.

Capt. M.: Yes, but I do remember when we were in out-of-the-way places, for instance, the ship went in to Cebu and the wardroom said we were all to go ashore to play golf, except for the duty section, and the top half of the ward room mess would challenge the lower half to a golf match. The junior man would play the senior man amd we'd work out ways in the middle. Then we would gather round, the steward's mates would take our/picnic lunch ashore for us and we went off and played golf in the morning, had a nice picnic lunch and some drinks, and golf in the afternoon for those who felt like it. And at occasions like that when we had just the officers around, the Captain would awlays be surrounded by a group of interested officers and he would tell his share of the stories and we would tell our share, or of our experiences and things when we would let him in on some of the things that went on in Tsingtao that he wasn't aware of or Chefoo, and that sort of thing. But I remember that he always enjoyed joining in a group of that sort and he welcomed the junior officers as well as the senior, and there was no hesitancy in an outlying place there when the families weren't present, or if the Captain were at the bar with the executive officer and two JOs came in, they were beckoned over to have a beer or a drink and they would roll for the drinks just like anyone else. The Captain always offered to pay. We always said, we'll roll, and we'll do our best to stick you. We didn't need any charity. But he was awfully good in that respect, and I don't think that people took advantage of his pleasantness and hospitality by being impudent or too forward. Frequently he went ashore. I remember in Tsingtao - Mrs. Nimitz did not come to Tsingtao one summer - and he walked a lot and he was always looking for somebody when his family wasn't there to walk with him, and he also played a lot of tennis with us JOs.

Q: Did you experience any one of those long walks?

Capt. M.: I never did because I always had something on as a JO, we'd always plan something ahead of time and he usually, in his walks, would take some of the senior officers who had not made any plans to go ashore. We JOs - before you went ashore you arranged something. Now, for instance, who would like to play tennis. Well, you'd find someone who wanted to play tennis, or play golf, or shall we go and have a few beers, or there's a good movie ashore, or I have a date, come on along, and we'll go dancing at the club. So, if you didn't have anything particularly planned, there was really not much sense in going ashore, because aboard ship we had a movie every night, if the weather permitted, the food in the ward room was very good, and you'd save money. Why get dressed up and go have a long, hot boat ride, and then have to catch a boat to get back. That was one of the problems of the bachelor officers, that a boat schedule had to be reasonable, you couldn't have the boat crew run all night, and yet you want to come home when you want to come home, and they want to get you off the streets when you want to get back to the ship, but the boats had schedules and they left on schedules, so we soon learned to regulate our lives to boat schedules. In China, with the sampans and the small boats, we were able to maneuver a little more independently. For instance, you could leave the Shanghai Club in the wee hours of the morning and take your date home in a taxi and have him take you down to the Whettimore Road jetty and get in a sampan and, for ten cents, be rowed out to the Augusta. And in our pidgin English, the Chinese of course, were of that caliber, didn't understand, so you'd say it was a two-piece bom-bom ship, a two-piece stack bom-bom ship. That meant it had two stacks and was a bom-bom ship which was a warship. Because there would be the President Coolidge or freighters or other ships along and if there was another warship from another country moored there at the Whettimore Road jetty, or in the Yangtze, called the Wangpoo, actually was the river off Shanghai. When taking a taxi for a dollar Chinese, which was about 25¢ at that exchange, you'd give the driver a small tip, 10 cents Chinese money, you'd get in a sampan for 10 or 15 cents, and in the sampan often would be the family. They'd be alseep under the floor boards, a mother and two children, and the father would row you out by oil lantern and drop you aboard ship, you'd give him the right amount of money. He tipped his hat and back he went to wait for someone else. So that made it a bit easy there. Some of the ports, particularly on our visits to strange ports, we were not familiar and we stuck to the boat schedule very closely. I played tennis with Captain Nimitz and Commander Whiting in Shanghai frequently. The French Club had beautiful lawn courts and of course in our tennis out there we had ball boys, so that your ball was put on your racket...

Q: Exercise was somewhat less.

Capt. M.: Well, you ran the ball to play it and that was the extent of the exercise.

Q: Did you have contact with him during World War II?

Capt. M.: The ship I was on went into Pearl Harbor to have propellors put on - the propellors had been damaged - and so I made a point of going to headquarters to see if he could see us, and he was delighted to see me and I spent ten minutes chatting with him. He was living with the other officers in a sort of bachelor quarters at the time - yes, up in Macalapa, and so I had about a ten-minute visit in his office up at CinCPac's headquarters, and that was all, but we were in for just two days. Then when he used to come back to Washington after he had retired, he didn't retire, but when he went back to live in Berkeley, I was administrative aide to Admiral Duncan who was Vice Chief of Naval Operations...

Q: Wu Duncan?

Capt. M.: Wu Duncan, yes.

Q: Were you really?

Capt. M.: ...for two years and when Nimitz would come back his office was right across from mine, which was next to the Vice Chief's office, and so I always saw him then and had little visits with him at that time. And that's when we would get him to dinner at our place or at the Levertons or something of that sort, when he was here for official visits and so forth.

Q: Did he seem somewhat different in his semi-retirement?

Capt. M.: No, I didn't think so. It was always first-name greeting to me and he would always ask about the Coxes and had Francis recovered from his experiences during the war, and how was my sister, Mary, and that was always flattering to have him remember and, actually, when my first daughter was born, we sent then Admiral Nimitz an announcement - that was in '45 - so she was born the latter part of World War II, he was still out in the Pacific fighting the war, and we got the nicest letter back "To Caroline", that was the young daughter, saying that he welcomed her and that he had known her Daddy and that he hoped that he would have the pleasure of taking her as a partner and beating my wife and me at tennis when this war was finished. So we framed that, and are very proud of that letter from Admiral Nimitz. It was that personal touch. After all, think of the hundreds of announcements of children arriving that he got, which would normally have been put in the waste basket or sent to Mrs. Nimitz or something of that sort. But for him to take the time to dictate a short note and refer to our tennis associations and so forth...

Q: One of the surprising things I've learned about him is his tremendous love for children. He spent hours and hours with children in his semi-retirement in Berkeley, hearkening to every beck and call, to every demand they might make of him.

When did you last see him?

Capt. M.: I guess it could have been - I was with Admiral Duncan '52 to '54, I guess it was, and that was probably the last time I saw him. Unless he came back after that and I was in and the Levertons would have me over because the Admiral was in town. And at one time, Junior and Katherine lived here and we went to their house for dinner one night when the Admiral was in town. When he came to Washington, if we were in town, one of our friends usually got hold of the Admiral and invited us all in to have a family dinner party, where just the people he had known, particularly out on the China Station in the Augusta, people stuck together very closely and...

Q: That seems to have been a red-letter cruise...

Capt. M.: It was, it certainly was, yes. And there again we were living aboard ship and we officers got to know each other very well. Leverton and I went back to the States in a destroyer together. Waters went to a destroyer building right alongside, so we were together in destroyers for a matter of two years in Norfolk, then out to the West Coast, and then we kind of separated and never served together again. In fact, the three of us came home on the President Coolidge together, and that was a memorable 18-day trip.

Q: I bet it was.

Capt. M.: No watches, and pretty girls, and we had a rather generous supply of liquor with us, we got it in Shanghai at a dollar a bottle.

Q: Just had a ball for 18 days.

Capt. M.: Yes. Then, too - now we got back, to show you how we thought of Nimitz, of the Captain, we got back to San Francisco, we'd been away from home over three years. We were all bachelors, our mothers were living then, and we wanted to get home, and the Bureau of Personnel, the 12th Naval District would not issue commercial orders across country, although we'd come from Shanghai to San Francisco commercially, because there was a transport in the area that was going around, andxwa which would have taken 30 days plus the delay in getting started, until they got word back from BuPers that permission was granted for comm ercial transportation. Well, we said, gee whizz, can we call on the telephone. The Chief of staff, 12th district, thought we'd lost our minds. We were staying at the Mark Hopkins Hotel, we were having a good time, but we wanted to get home first, so we said, well, the only thing to do is to get hold of Nimitz. So we sent him a telegram and signed it "Leverton, Waters, Moncure - please expedite comm ercial transportation San Francisco to Washington. Com 12 won't grant until you authorize." Well that was the day his son graduated from the Naval Academy and he was at Annapolis, and his secretary got this thing and she knew that there'd been a Moncure in China and that was a magic word in BuPers at that time in his office, but there was SP and a JP, and no LW, and somebody else came in and said, "Oh, hell, that's Muddy and Bill and Sam." So they immediately sent a priority dispatch to Com 12 authorizing commercial transportation for the three of us. Well, we went in the next morning to check with the Chief of Staff to see whether our transportation....He didn't send the request until the morning this message arrived, so he wanted to know what we had done, and you've never seen such innocent lambs in your life. But we got our tickets that day and were out of San Francisco in the next hour. He was delighted. He used to joke about that period, and, gosh, if you want something done, go to the top man. But I'm sure he did the same things for other shipmates on the Augusta and we all didn't hesitate to call on him and had he called on us, we would have risen to the occasion, too.

Q: Yes, the group on the Augusta and also the men - the Reserves - who were at Berkeley in '26 when he was out there setting up this prototype NROTC, this also was a red-letter thing...

Capt. M.: Yes, he spoke of it - he loved Berkeley and he was very proud of his ROTC, NROTC, unit and I'm glad he can't see what's happening at Berkeley now. It would break his heart. Because we just don't understand - I don't understand things like that, and he would have more trouble than I do.

Q: What is your estimate of him as a man?

Capt. M.: Oh, I thought he was straightforward, he was honest as the day is long, and he certainly had humility. He was not a bragger or demanding respect for being the captain of the ship, and yet nobody ever failed to give him complete respect. So that - I don't know how to express it, but he had that certain amount of aloofness which is due to dignity and ability, and that's the impression, I think, that all the men in the ship had of him too. You'll occasionally see where the crew are a little disrespectful towards a captain in the presence of junior officers and so forth. We never experienced that with Captain Nimitz. I don't ever remember a crewman being smart alecky or disrespectful towards him in somebody else's presence, and I think that was inherited and throughout the ship. There again, the *Augusta* had a peculiar arrangement - two years with practically no transfers. The men grew together, and the good men were promoted, the poor ones were demoted, and we got rid of some, we sent some to gaol, we sent some home for better assignment. We were always delighted when we could get a man off for officer candidate school or opportunities of that sort, or sent back for a better assignment, and that was unusual to have a ship where the officers and the crew had such a small turnover. Because all of us who went out in the ship had the commanders and above serve two years, and the rest of us three years, and about 10 per cent volunteered to stay on for - I beg your pardon, two years and two and a half, and some volunteered to stay for that extra six months. Herbie Coleman was one and I think Courtney Shands was another.

Q: Well, that's all very interesting, Sir.

Capt. M.: I'm sorry that I don't remember some of his little stories, anecdotes...

Q: I would like to have one or two. I've been trying to make a collection of them.

Capt. M.: Yes. I must confess that my memory isn't good

enough to recall them.

Q: I would suspect, perhaps, that he blossomed forth as a storyteller in his latter years. That this is when he took great pleasure in collecting them.

Capt. M.: Well, truthfully, I don't remember any stories, so that could be that he just did not tell any in my presence. Now, we used to sit around the porch at the Army and Navy Country Club over a beer, after tennis, when some of the ladies would join us, and he liked to talk, he liked to tell of a little experience here and a little experience there, but he never monopolized the conversation and wanted to be talking all the time. He wanted to hear what other people had to say, too. And he was interested in the younger lives. The Levertons - Helen Leverton produced twins for him - twin girls - and the Nimitzes and we went down to see them off to fly to Atlanta when they had these two twins in a big laundry basket to go on an Eastern Air Lines tri-motored plane out of the old airport in Washington, and I had a picture of that I saw the other day, but the twins weren't there, so I didn't think it would be of great significance. Two little girls and Helen were going down to her home to visit her family, and Nimitz was just as concerned about those little girls as you can imagine. More so than Helen was. He wanted to make sure she had enough food for them and all that sort of business.

INDEX

for an interview

with

CAPTAIN SAMUEL P. MONCURE, U. S. NAVY (RET.)

Alabama, 14

Athletic endeavors, 12-14

Augusta, 1-5, 15, 17-21, 25, 29, 31, 34, 37, 39-40

Barton, 20

Bermerton Navy Yard, 1-2, 5

Blackhawk, 24

Cebu Bay, 26

Chinese coolie labor, 3-5

Coleman, Herbert, 20, 40

Duncan, Admiral Donald B., 35, 37

Freckles, (family dog) 31

Gygax, Captain Felix Xerxes, 17

Henderson, 9, 29

Hill, Commander Kitchen, 24-25

Houston, 2-5, 19

Iltus Hook, 6, 17

Ingersoll, Captain Royall, 1-2

Japanese, 10-11

Lamar, Lt. Howell A., 14

Lay, Catherine (Nimitz) 15, 17

Lay, James, 15, 17

Leverton, Helen, 41

Leverton, LT Joseph Wilson, 13-14, 16, 36-37

Manila: Asiatic Fleet base, 6-7, 12, 14, 17, 21, 29

Mast, 22-23

Mohan, Dick, 20

Mustin, Admiral Lloyd, 19-20

Neutrality Partol, 13-14, 29

Nimitz, Catherine, (see Lay) ~~15, 17~~

Nimitz, Mrs. Chester W., 30

Nimitz, Chester W. Jr., 15

Nimitz, Nancy, 15

USS *President Coolidge*, 17-18

Puller, General Chester, 23

Richardson, Captain J. O., 1-2

Shands, Courtney, 40

Shanghai, 3, 5, 8-9, 15, 17, 27, 34-35, 37

Soochow, 6

State Department, 9

Tsingtao; Asiatic Fleet base, 6-8, 12, 33

Tucker, 29

Upham, Admiral F. B., 3

Waters, Admiral Odale D. Jr., 16, 37

Whiting, CDR F. E. M., 13, 15, 17, 24-25, 35

DECLARATION OF TRUST

The undersigned does hereby appoint and designate as his (her) Trustee herein, the Secretary-Treasurer and Publisher of the United States Naval Institute to perform and discharge the following duties, powers, and privileges in connection with the possession and use of a certain taped interview between the undersigned and the Oral History Department of the United States Naval Institute.

(1) As an <u>Open</u> transcript it may be read (or the tape audited) by qualified researchers upon presentation of proper credentials as determined by the Trustee. In the case of interviews about the late Fleet Admiral C. W. Nimitz, it is intended that first use of the material shall be made by the biographer of the Fleet Admiral, Professor E. B. Potter, and the Naval Institute is authorized to deal with the material in this fashion.

(2) It is expressly understood that in giving this authorization, I am in no way precluded from placing such restrictions as I may desire upon use of the interview at any time during my lifetime, nor does this authorization in any way affect my rights to the copyright of any literary expressions that may be contained in the interview.

Witness my hand and seal this 23rd day of June 1970

[signature]
VAdm US Navy

I hereby accept and consent to the foregoing Declaration of Trust and the powers therein conferred upon me as Trustee:

[signature]
Secretary-Treasurer and Publisher

Interview with Vice Admiral Lloyd M. Mustin, U.S. Navy

Place: His office in DASA Headquarters, Arlington, Virginia.

Subject: Fleet Admiral Chester W. Nimitz.

Date, Tuesday morning, 10 March 1970

By: John T. Mason, Jr.

Q: Admiral Mustin, it's awfully kind of you to see me and give me in this fashion your recollections of the late Fleet Admiral Chester Nimitz. Would you begin by telling me about your first meeting with him?

Adm. M.: Yes, and I suppose I could carry that through as a sort of a resume of my whole career of knowing him as a framework into which to fit anything else that you want to go into.

Q: All right, Sir.

Adm. M.: I graduated from the Naval Academy in 1932 and was assigned to the heavy cruiser Augusta (CA-31), one of the very fine so-called Treaty cruisers. She was quite new at that time, and representing several substantial advances in fighting capability and speed flexibility and so on...

Q: And with all, quite a beautiful...

Adm. M.: Oh, yes...over the majority of the Navy of the day, which were mainly leftover World War I relics. Anyway, this was a very fine ship at that time, really a leader in every area of competition, gunnery, athletics, engineering, anything, all placed near the top of the pile. The captain was James O. Richardson and he, needless to say, set very high standards. Captain Richardson had put the ship in commission in about February of 1931, I think, and had her up until about the summer of '33. He was relieved temporarily by Admiral R. E. Ingersoll - Captain R. E. Ingersoll, of course, at that time - briefly. Captain Ingersoll was slated to go to another heavy cruiser still under construction, and this was recognized as an interim assignment for him, with Captain Nimitz to relieve him after just a few months. And Captain Nimitz relieved in, as I recall it, the late summer of 1933. The ship was the flagship of the Scouting Force, at that time a three-star command. This had delayed her entry into the Navy Yard for scheduled overhaul, because no other flagship was available, and consequently we went in the Navy Yard in about September to accomplish in two months what had been planned as a three-month overhaul preparatory for leaving for the Asiatic Station for an indefinitely extended tour, and it was at about the time of the start of that, that Captain Nimitz came on board.

Q: This was in Bremerton, wasn't it?

Adm. M.: The overhaul was in Bremerton. Because of the considerable climate of economy at that time, the plan was to send her to the China Station with essentially a complete crew of people whose normal sea duty tours would leave them on board for the full normal China tour, which at that time, was three years. This meant that besides the general turbulence of the Navy Yard overhaul, and the particular turbulence of a delay in it and a compression of it, all superimposed upon the fact that it was going to be the last one in the States for a long time, on top of that came a very large-scale turnover of the crew and an almost complete turnover of all the officers, excepting for us ensigns who were looking forward to six or seven year initial tour at sea anyway and could therefore safely be left on board to go out to China.

This is what Captain Nimitz came into. He made himself felt in ways that I like to talk about, and will to whatever extent you want, but for purposes of this outline, we completed that overhaul successfully, we sailed for China on time, on schedule. The incidents and adventures out there were legion, and he had the ship for approximately two years, and left her out there to go home to duty in the Bureau of Navigation. I stayed in her.

He seemed to have taken a particular interest in the group of ensigns. Actually, although it was a heavy cruiser, as I recall it we only had about 35 officers in the ship, as compared to the 100-and some you would find in a heavy cruiser these days.

Q: That was due, perhaps, to the height of the Depression, was it and in the lack of funds?

Adm. M.: No, this was not an artificially compressed number. This was the peace-time number that was thought appropriate for a ship of that kind. This was not the war complement of officers, but it was the proper peacetime number, and we had on board more officers and more men because of our distant deployment than the average in the States. Even so, it was a relatively small family, and in that family we ensigns felt that we were in a particularly favorable position to be given responsibilities and to discharge them effectively, because we were the old-timers in the ship, you see, we were the only ones who hadn't been swept out...

Q: You were the continuity.

Adm. M.: Yes. In any case, we all certainly felt that Admiral Nimitz - Captain Nimitz - took a very strong personal interest in us all, and I suppose that's one of the universal attributes of anybody who's ever served with him. I've never heard anything different. But, in any case, he left to go home to the Bureau of Navigation, predecessor of the Bureau of Personnel, and before leaving he had considerable to say to us by way of career advice, what we should seek to do next, which was to go not only to destroyers, as a change in type of Navy ship, but to the new construction ones, which were then beginning to be built, as a break in the famine from the old World War I 1,200-tonners.

And so, indeed, all of us having gone out together with the ship, all of us came due for normal rotation home at about the same time; all of us asked for new destroyers; and obviously thanks to his management back here in Washington, all of us went to them. I went to one that was building up in Maine, the Lamson (DD-367), building in Bath, Maine, which went in commission in October 1936. She went out to the West Coast, was home-ported in San Diego, operated in and out of San Diego.

From the time Captain Nimitz left the *Augusta* on to the end of his life, my contacts with him were quite random, remotely spaced I suppose, fairly infrequent and brief, and they went something like this. He left that shore duty assignment in the Bureau of Navigation to come back to the Fleet, almost all of which was on the West Coast in those days. In my recollection, he had by now been promoted to Rear Admiral, and he had command of a Light Cruiser Division based in San Diego. Their operations followed one pattern and ours a different one, so that opportunities for encounters were not too frequent, but those encounters were always in the same old pattern: Great cordiality, instantaneous recognition, affectionate comments, and so on. For example, the Nimitzes...

Q: As though there had been no interim?

Adm. M.: As though there were no interlude and that we were still working for him. Now this was a very profound feeling that I always had that I always was working for him. Maybe because it was all one Navy or something. He liked an athletic, outdoor type of life, and as likely as not, you would run into the Nimitz family at the swimming pool there, at the Hotel del Coronado. There we would be, there we would meet them, and there'd always be a brief conversation in passing, you know, "How are the children?" and this sort of thing. Very pleasant.

I left that destroyer out there in the summer of '38 and went back East to the postgraduate school, which was a nominal three-year course, from which I went to a new construction light cruiser, the Atlanta (CL-51), the first of the so-called antiaircraft light cruisers, building in the East. She went in commission in December 1941, had her shake-down cruise in the Atlantic, went through the Canal and out to the Pacific in about March of '42, and, of course, went from Panama direct, nonstop, to Honolulu, Pearl Harbor, and by this time Admiral Nimitz had taken command of the Pacific Fleet and had a war on his hands.

I had a number of encounters with his senior staff, although I was only a lieutenant, in some general matters of interest to them concerning this new type of ship. I was the Assistant Gunnery Officer. There was a considerable interest in their gunnery capabilities and so on, and, of course, this led to just sort of a courtesy call in his office. And here was this four-star admiral, sitting there running the toughest war that our Navy has ever fought, I guess, and yet one of his, to me, very senior staff officers - might be a commander or even a captain - would say, "Well, the old man wants to see you before you go," and I'd just go in and sit down and have a cup of coffee, and again there would be, "Where is Emily?" and "Where are the children?" and he knew all their names, he never forgot a name.

Just a thoroughly remarkable personal impact that came through from that man.

My stepfather, George Murray, was commanding officer of the Enterprise at that time, and after the Tokyo raid, Admiral Nimitz presented him and a large number of others with some combat decorations in a ceremony held on the flight deck of the Enterprise. The Atlanta was in port and I was able to be present at the ceremony, and, of course here was another brief contact with Admiral Nimitz.

The Atlanta operated in and out of there. We were in the Battle of Midway, came back in to Pearl Harbor after that, did a little refitting and additional gunnery training, and routine things, and finally sailed in August for the invasion of Guadalcanal...

Q: May I interrupt?

Adm. M.: Yes.

Q: Did the Admiral himself inspect the Atlanta, it being a new type ship?

Adm. M.: I am very hesitant about that. I just don't remember. If anybody told me that he had, I would assume it as perfectly natural, but I couldn't testify to it in a court of law. We were just so busy. We had a new ship, new type, problems – some of our equipment was giving us trouble, and it was my business to get it fixed, and there wasn't any time for amenities. And yet, he would take them, you know. If I would be up in the Headquarters, for example, talking to the Fleet Gunnery Officer about these problems, this would be the sort of fellow who would say, "Now, the old man wants you to stop in for a minute," and I would.

Well, the Atlanta went to the South Pacific and she was sunk down there in November, and I landed on Guadalcanal as one of the survivors, and I got assigned there to duty on the island and stayed for - oh, until about February of '43. I got off the island into a sister ship of the

Mustin - 8

Atlanta that was operating down there in the area, the San Diego. Stayed in her until that summer when I came home to the States and put another new construction ship in commission, the Miami, a 6-inch light cruiser, CL-89, I guess, building, again, on the East Coast. She shook down on the East Coast, and when she was ready she went West. So, here I was again, for the first time in a long time, back in Pearl Harbor in the early spring of '43. We weren't in any longer than it took to reload with ammunition and go West. I don't think I saw Admiral Nimitz then, meaning I hadn't seen him since the summer of '42.

I stayed in that ship all through the Marianas Campaign, the Marshalls, Gilberts Campaign, and finally, about the time we were starting to work over the Philippines, I was transferred at sea to the staff of Vice Admiral Willis A. Lee, who was Commander, Battleships, Pacific Fleet, the second-in-command of the Third Fleet, and, I guess, had a few other assorted operational jobs. One of these high-line transfers at sea, to his staff, in about November of '44.

Q: That was a rather unusual thing, wasn't it, to be transferred at sea?

Adm. M.: One thing that seemed unusual to me then, and still does, was to go to the staff of the type commander of battleships, which he was amongst other things, never having served a day's duty in my life as a ship's officer in a battleship, and never have since.

In any case, he was one of the very senior and very experienced combat commanders in the Pacific. So somewhere along there in the fall of '44 Admiral Lee's flagship, the South Dakota, went into dry dock in Guam to have some underwater damage repaired, and of course Admiral Lee had immediate and frequent contacts and, I'm sure, lengthy discussions with Admiral Nimitz about what was to be done, what were our capabilities, and so forth. And I, as his gunnery officer and radar officer and Combat Information Center officer, was one of his principal staff assistants in these operational and planning discussions; and here again, for the first time in a couple of years, I had brief and quite familiar encounters with Admiral Nimitz.

After the Okinawa Campaign, the war was pretty well along, and, I'm talking something like June '45, the invasion of Japan was very much in the front of everyone's mind out there. Plans were being drawn, operations were getting under way. Admiral King brought Admiral Lee home to found what's now called the Operational Test and Evaluation Force. At that point in time, its purpose was to take a real quick look through the eyes of combat experienced, operational-type, seagoing naval officers, at all kinds of new developments which were pouring out of the laboratories, all of which were, of course, being advocated by their particular enthusiasts as the absolute answer to how to win the war, how to invade Japan with minimum losses, and all of that. The purpose was to pick and choose among these. There was such a plethora of them that I think Admiral King simply felt that there wasn't any organization in Washington whose judgment he could rely on to pick the ones we should concentrate on getting out to the fleet for the invasion of Japan. That's what Admiral

Lee's job was, and Admiral Lee brought me home with him.

Q: As it was partially your job, too?

Adm. M.: Well, the items of most immediate interest were indeed gunnery, radar, and Combat Information Center items, and Admiral Lee knew I'd been out there all through the war, working with those matters. We left the flagship in Leyte Gulf, came home by air, stopping in Guam for one day conferring with Admiral Nimitz, and again I had just a brief personal encounter.

Q: Did his attitude change at that point?

Adm. M.: No change perceptible to me. The same person...

Q: I mean in terms of the war. I mean, was he being highly optimistic, at that point?

Adm. M.: No. Perfectly factual. I think he saw it very clearly from our point of view.

For example, my boss at that time, Admiral Lee, had gone out from duty in Washington at about the time the South Dakota was put in commission a new fast battleship. The Washington and the North Carolina were the first two. The North Carolina was sent to the Pacific in the summer of '42 - I remember the excitement when she arrived. The Washington, which had been operating with the British against the Tirpitz and so on came out later. The South Dakota was the third of these, they formed a division, and Admiral Lee went out there as the commander of that battleship division, arriving down in the far South Pacific at Tonga Tabu, in the fall of '42, and he had never been home since. The farthest to the rear he had ever been since going down to the South Pacific in the South Dakota in '42 was back as far as Pearl Harbor. So he had been in Pearl Harbor or forward of there ever since the fall of '42, and he was a thoroughly knowledgeable man about what was what in the Pacific, what our capabilities were, what our shortcomings were. He had a good professional mind. He had great depth of professional curiosity and a considerable technical bent. He understood what were then new things, like radar and influence fuses and so on.

Admiral Nimitz knew that. I guess Admiral King knew it - that's why Admiral King said, "Lee is the man. Bring him back." Admiral Lee had a pretty realistic appraisal of what the war amounted to. His staff was very small, I suppose about 15 officers. As the second-in-command of the Third Fleet he had access to the most closely held information, intelligence, and everything else planned, and we, the operating officers of his staff, had it also.

Anyway, I thought that there was a beautiful coherence observable between everything we knew or thought we knew, or saw or thought we saw, out in the frontlines where we were shooting the guns in anger nearly every day of our lives, and the way things were understood at Admiral Nimitz' headquarters.

On our part, toward his headquarters there was none of this "What do those stupid bastards back there think they're doing?" you know, that was so characteristic of our appraisals of some of what was going on in Washington. There was no such hiatus between the people in the front lines and the understandings that were reflected from Admiral Nimitz' headquarters.

There was no question but that there was a very close and real understanding of what was going on, and of what lay ahead. There was no cause for fatuous optimism about what lay ahead. We didn't know for sure how tough it was, but we had some pretty good ideas about how tough it could be and probably was going to be.

Q: Admiral, that close understanding, would you dissect it, a bit, would you analyze it? It was based on...

Adm. M.: Well, perhaps the best way to do it is to give you a few examples. The Pacific Fleet survived in those operations against Japan because of its ability to withstand Japanese counter efforts, which were probably the most dangerous by air. I'm not discounting the Japanese surface effectiveness at all, but...

Q: It was formidable, at times, wasn't it?

Adm. M.: Initially, the Pacific was a Japanese lake. There's no doubt about it. They went where they chose, when they chose, and it was pretty bad to be in their way, and we went in their way. It wasn't easy, but after the so-called Marianas Turkey Shoot in June '44, it seemed pretty clear that now it was a United States lake. We could go wherever we chose. Their fleet withdrew and looked for opportunities to catch us with our guard down or something, as exampled by their sortie against us in Leyte Gulf.

But after we got on the offensive their most dangerous weapon to us was their aviation. The combination of their fleet air flying off the carriers, their fleet air flying off of land bases, which they did very skillfully, coordinated very well with their carrier-based air, and their land-based Army aviation, which was never really as much of a threat. It was their naval aviation that was dangerous then.

Well, our ability to do what we did was measured by our ability to beat their air. Their most dangerous efforts against our fleet were by air while we were delivering our choice of blows against them - sinking their ships by submarine, landing Marines, landing 16-inch naval gun projectiles on their territory, landing Marines on their territory, and landing a lot of bombs on their territory from our own naval aviation - that pretty soon made it possible to land the bombs from the B-29s on Japan.

The Fleet's ability to survive their air offensive against it, of course, was a measure of the combination of every element of air defense, the outermost one being our own aviation striking his aircraft on their fields, or sinking his aircraft carriers from which the aircraft came, and so forth. But those measures were never air tight, and they were always able to get off some strikes against you. You meet them first and farthest out with your own aviation, positioned and controlled by radar - detect the incoming Japanese, vector your own fighters out there, and start shooting them down, à la Marianas Turkey Shoot. In this function, of course the heart and soul, the key to the whole thing, was our radar.

We were having some pretty good successes with certain kinds of radars out there, which gave us the kind and quality of information we needed, when, lo and behold, we found that the people back in Washington didn't think that was the right kind of radar. It didn't have certain features they thought radar should have, and they were going to provide us with their idea of the right kind of radar. Well, people out where we were were a little cautious about this, about giving up what they had that they knew worked, and substituting for it something that was relatively new and untried, merely because "Father knew best" in Washington.

When some of the things that "Father knew best" about turned out not to work, this was pretty bad because here were the ships 7,000 miles from any place you could fix it, with radar that just wouldn't do the job. But we never felt this kind of difference of understanding between the front lines and Admiral Nimitz.

Q: There were plenty of examples in the realm of ordnance, weren't there, where this was true?

Adm. M.: Yes, this was going to be my next comment. The big killer of incoming aircraft that got through the fighters were the 5-inch guns with the so-called VT fuze, the influence fuze. Well, my postgraduate training in the Navy was in fire control, my particular applications of it had been in the antiaircraft world. I've probably had as much or more antiaircraft experience, including shots fired in anger, than anybody you can find or identify from the USN. Problems were pretty clear to me, and to all who knew what they were doing and understood what they were doing, I think they were quite equally clear.

It's difficult to set a mechanical time fuze accurately to cause it to detonate the shell where you need it to, in the very close vicinity of an aircraft, if you're really going to kill it with that detonation. The lethal volume of a bursting 5-inch shell is, in fact, quite small. The influence fuze takes care of the toughest part of that problem for you. It lets the shell go on until it gets to its closest point, and then it triggers it...

Q: It, in effect, does its own thinking.

Adm. M.: Does its own fuze-setting, and everyone out there was convinced that the influence fuze was the greatest single advance in antiaircraft effectiveness almost since the invention of the antiaircraft gun, and I'm prepared to believe that.

In any case, we started the war without them, we didn't have them. The first ones were used in anger in about February '43, down in the South Pacific, and they left a great deal to be desired. They were electronic. They got their electric power from dry-cell batteries, batteries with limited life. As the numbers of these VT-fuzed shells came pouring out of the States, and the numbers in the Fleet grew from the hundreds to the thousands to the tens and hundreds of thousands, the fuze battery

Mustin - 16

problem began to be a serious one. Well, other characteristics to that fuze were troublesome, too.

But we had become aware of the Japanese kamikaze tactic. It manifested itself sporadically, I guess, as early as early '43, but it was quite obviously a planned and organized chosen tactic by the time of '44.

With a kamikaze, the plane you had to shoot down was one who was going to get as close to you as he could get, preferably crashing on the deck, and if you hadn't killed him or torn him to shreds, you were interested in continuing to try to do that until the last instant before he landed on board. So we were quite concerned with the innermost range at which these VT fuzes could be armed, and the fuzes in production and being delivered to us seemed reasonably satisfactory with respect to this feature. The inner arming range was sort of random, there was a rather wide distribution, but by and large it was all right. It was good enough. We weren't complaining.

Lo and behold, we learned to our stunned dismay that "Father knew best" back here in Washington. He didn't know what was going on in the war, but in search of a different category of improvement in the VT fuze, which he claimed to have accomplished, he gave us a fuze that had an inner arming range that was three or four times farther out than what we already had. This was almost beyond belief, really, to the people out there whose lives were on the line every day, and whose defense was to tear those people apart so they couldn't fly on to you. To be given a fuze that took away from you a capability that you'd been using every day, and you counted on in order to stay alive, it was beyond belief, and yet this was the sort of thing that came out of Washington, you know. No bother, no strain - "You all just don't understand."

Q: They had improved upon it and...

Adm. M.: Yes. This was the sort of thing - in every area, this kind of unbelievable mis-estimation of what the Fleet really needed - that seemed to be coming out of Washington. There were no counterparts whatsoevever of that coming out of Nimitz' headquarters.

ONI was blandly telling us that the Yamato and the Musashi couldn't possibly have larger than 16-inch guns. You know there were rumors seeping into the intelligence channels from other sources that these might be 45 centimeter guns, which would be 18-inch guns. Just from looking at the photography, I said that there's nothing whatsoever there that says that's not an 18-inch gun, and I happened to have seen an 18-inch gun. The U.S. Navy built some in late World War I days, and we'd had one down in Dahlgren, so I'd seen 18-inch guns. There's nothing there that says that's not an 18-inch gun, and we had better remain alert to the fact that those ships may be armed, indeed, with guns of that caliber. This was accepted forthwith in CinCPacFlt's intelligence family. Not so, Washington.

Washington perpetrated on the U.S. Navy at that time that gray uniform. Nimitz never took off his khakis, and furthermore, you know, the regulation book said, "Well, all right, everybody who owns khaki can continue to wear them until not only have you worn out your own but until the supply of them in the pipeline is exhausted." Well, somehow or other, Nimitz arranged that the pipeline to the Pacific never got exhausted.

Q: And yet that uniform was purported to have been the idea of Admiral King himself!

Adm. M.: It was, so I heard. But it's funny how little things like that matter.

You know, we sort of lived in the tropics, and gosh, when you finally get down below after all day on the water in the tropical sun, and sunburnt no matter what you could do about it -- cheeks, nose, and lips always blistered and peeled -- it was good to get a chance to get down below, clean up, get a bath, put on a nice clean uniform. And khaki looked clean, and it was cool and so on. The gray looked messy, streaked, and had a dreary connotation about it, and people out there just didn't like it.

Well, it was perfectly obvious that neither did Nimitz, and here was the "to heck with those shore duty guys back in Washington, we're going to wear khaki. The boss wears khaki." An intangible little thing.

Well, of course, the ramifications were almost ludicrous, because pretty soon, all of those who'd been there in the Fleet were wearing khakis, but some newcomer, just newly out from shore duty in Washington, would show up in gray. Well, this would mark him as a newcomer, and this was not good for his morale, so he'd be around beating the bushes trying to find himself some khaki uniforms.

When we got back here to Washington, Admiral Lee and two or three of his staff that he'd brought with him to start this OpDepFor thing, we all had pretty scanty and shabby outfits of uniforms, so Admiral Lee had an invitations to dinner at the White House or something and he needed a new uniform, so he sent me and others out beating the bushes, where could he get a uniform and it had to be khaki. He wasn't going to wear a gray uniform. Well, the tailors were all very apologetic. The run on khaki was just beyond their ability to keep up with, because everybody - the war was nearing its end, you know, and everybody in Washington had to rush out to get his Legion of Merit or something like that quickly before it was too late, so naturally they had the word and they were all buying themselves outfits of khaki uniforms to take to the Pacific.

Q: Almost two navies in terms of uniform.

Adm. M.: Yes. Well, in any case, we've been talking at some length here on elaborating on our feeling -- I'll say, my feeling from a position of access to considerable highly classified information and considerable privileged information, - that Admiral Nimitz' appreciation of the war, where we stood, what we'd done, what remained to be done, was absolutely and thoroughly realistic. I can certainly say that nobody ever heard from him any expressions of hesitancy about proceeding, getting ahead with the job that had to be done, we're going to do it, and here's the time schedule, here's what's planned, and this is what we're going to do. I'm sure nobody ever heard any expressions of fatuous optimism or thoughtless or unjustified discounting of the fairly substantial dangers that lay ahead, and ex post facto, of course, we know that there were very real dangers.

Q: And surprises!

Adm. M.: Yeah. For example, the intelligence community kept estimating their air order of battle as, let's say, 4,000 aircraft by that time. When we actually got on the ground in Japan, we found that there were nearly double the number that had been estimated. They had kept them very carefully concealed. They had kept them out of any operational employment that would reveal their numbers, and they kept them concealed such that aerial photographic reconnaissance wouldn't find them. So, here we would have been, going in against double the number of aircraft that the estimations had identified.

But those who were looking at the upcoming job were, I think, fairly realistically aware that the information was simply not reliable enough to permit one to discount the possibility of things of this nature. And many other things. Some of them might have worked, some might have worked partially, some of them didn't have a chance. There was a desperation scheme, as you know, last-ditch efforts of the Japanese...

Q: Well, the kamikaze itself was a prime example of that.

Adm. M.: Yes, it was.

Mustin - 21

Q: Also, in the same vein, the frequent trips which Admiral Nimitz took to the various islands and so forth, was the cause of this wasn't it?

Adm. M.: Lots of contact with his responsible operational commanders, so that he knew what they saw and what they thought and how they felt about things, and they knew what he knew, and they knew what he knew about what lay ahead, what kind of support we were going to be able to get from back home. Really -- well, let me jump ahead a bit to wind up this outline. We've sort of gotten into some of the internal details unintentionally...

Q: That's inevitable.

Adm. M.: Yes. After the war, I remained briefly in that Operational Test and Evaluation Force with Admiral Lee, left it in...

Q: Did that prove effective, as a technique?

Adm. M.: It did, indeed. This would be difficult to document, because we were under such a press of urgency that most of our decisions were made sort of by the seat of the pants on the spot, given by telephone to Washington and action was taken accordingly. Admiral Burke, who had been - as a Commodore - Admiral Mitscher's chief of staff, was brought back here to run an office in the Pentagon that had to do with supporting the Fleet in the Western Pacific. He was our contact...

Mustin - 22

Q: This is Arleigh Burke?

Adm. M.: Yes. Mainly by telephone. We welcomed with open arms anything and everything that they had to offer. We found ways to try it out to our satisfaction. Had an assorted stable of ships. We had the old Wyoming which had been a gunnery training ship, and we had new construction ships that were brand new, never heard a shot fired in anger, had a cross section of people in them, some from the Pacific, many from the Atlantic, where the war was essentially over. They were delayed before deploying, to work with us and test assorted bits and pieces of equipment, just to give us test platforms. We had three squadrons of aircraft of our own, all piloted by pilots who had a minimum of three combat tours in the Pacific, so they were sleekly expert combat veterans and could reproduce any set of hypothetical tactics that you wanted.

We just worked all day every day, seven days a week, and came to some conclusions possibly many of them representing some preconceived notions or some snap judgments, but there wasn't time to do any more. That's the way we did it. When the war ended, the force apparently had proved itself to the satisfaction of responsible people. It was continued and it exists today. They do things now, of course, on a much more orderly basis, maybe a little bit too orderly in that their pace of operations is constrained by normal peacetime operating schedules...

Q: The pressures are lifted.

Adm. M.: Yes. If they want to do a very scientifically precise evaluation on the basis of data recorded in operations, this immediately bespeaks a stretched-out time to accomplish this evaluation and get it all written into a very highly formalized report, and it takes too long. It takes longer than you'd like to take. We weren't able to seek that scientific quality in the prose of our reports, the erudite style, the scientific precision in our data, or the length of time required to do it. We were sort of shooting from the hip.

Q: There are probably too many channels now.

Adm. M.: In retrospect, though, I think -- as is easily said, not so easily documented - we had feelings of profound responsibility for what we did. I felt it at that time. We didn't do anything lightly. We knew what the stakes were, and I recall in retrospect a feeling of responsibility for what we did.

I don't recall a single instance of anything that we said "go," that in hindsight we would have given a different recommendation. Nor, on the other side of the coin, can I recall anything we said, "that won't cut the mustard, don't try to deploy it," where later events didn't prove that to be right.

An example of the latter, everyone felt it would be terribly important if our shipboard radars could have a feature known in the jargon as "moving target indication" (MTI), meaning that as the radar scans around and around, targets that stand still have their successive echoes compared in opposition and cancel each other out, whereas if between scans the target has moved a little, cancellation does not occur and you see the target. So you see only those that are moving. If you were off an invasion beach, for example, with this feature at work, the land which ordinarily would be a source of a great smear on the radar screen, blanking out any hope of detecting aircraft, would not be moving, so it wouldn't show. So if an aircraft came in, for example, try to kamikaze you, you'd get radar detection on him, even though he'd come over the land.

So we were given what was supposed to be a modification to go into one of the then widely deployed Navy shipboard radars, the SG, which hopefully and theoretically would give it this MTI capability. We slapped it into a ship and hooked it all up, and we had the benefit of all the protagonists and proponents of this thing, from its inventors on down, to help tune this thing up.

But we never could make it work, and we formed our own seat-of-the-pants conclusions as to why we were not able to make it work, with, to be honest, the sincere advice of all of the enthusiasts and others. So I went and described these things to Admiral Lee, and he picked up the phone to Arleigh Burke and said it's no go, and not only does it not do what it's supposed to do, but it adds these penalties of complexity and loss of reliability to the basic unmodified radar, and I just don't think we can afford to have it aboard the ships, and my recommendation is, no. And that killed it.

Q: Burke understood your language, too, did he?

Mustin - 25

Adm. M.: Absolutely, and he had complete faith in Lee. The whole "Father knows best" radar empire in Washington was sort of staking its reputation on this one. This was going to win the war, and when this bombshell hit Washington, why, Arleigh got into a plane and came up there to talk to Lee face to face.

Q: Where were you?

Adm. M.: Casco Bay. We were operating out of Casco Bay. We'd taken this thing on up to some of the higher ground areas close to Maine and tried it against flat land backgrounds, mountain backgrounds, but it wouldn't work. Couldn't make it work. So Arleigh was persuaded, and that decision stuck, and the fact of the matter was the Navy never did succeed in providing an MTI to those radars.

Q: How fortunate that you didn't have to learn this in wartime!

Adm. M.: We couldn't have afforded to learn it at sea in the war zone. Well, that story is another diversion.

I came ashore to Washington in March of '46. I was here, then, during the period, briefly, when Admiral Nimitz was CNO. I was here from '46 to '48, in the Bureau of Ordnance. I saw him, as far as I can remember, only once. I was a very junior cog in the big machine. I went to his office for a presentation of an award to Dr. Draper - Charles Stark Draper, the inertial guidance genius. Stark Draper had been one of my professors at MIT, and he'd been associated with me there in a development that he made for antiaircraft fire control. It was in relation to that that this award was being given him. And so, lo and behold, not having seen Admiral Nimitz since some place 7,000 miles from...

Q: On Guam.

Adm. M.: The whole World War II conclusion away, why, here was the same very friendly personal greetings, a few comments referring back to old times and old places.

I next saw him after he had retired and was living there in the Berkeley area. I had command of a destroyer squadron, and half of it, the division which included my flagship, went into the Hunter's Point Navy Yard for a regular overhaul. While we were there, the Thetis Bay which had been a World War II escort carrier, baby flattop, had been taken out of mothballs and modified somewhat to be a helicopter carrier, in loose terms, an assault helicopter for operation in the amphibious forces. And she was the first of her kind. She inaugurated this new concept, which we are still following in a big way in the amphibious forces today.

She was commissioned at the Hunter's Point Navy Yard on a bitterly cold day in, I would suppose, the late fall of '56 or early spring of '57, and Admiral Nimitz was the principal speaker.

Well, the ceremony was on the flight deck of this carrier, and the flight deck was absolutely jammed. The guest list included everybody important from naval aviation, everybody important from the Marine Corps, everybody important from the amphibious force, everybody important from the political-military community that concerns itself with Navy programs, and everybody interested in the start of a highly new class of ship. It was a mob scene. Admiral Nimitz was the principal speaker, and after the ceremony there was a reception there in the officers' club. The receiving line must have had a thousand people in it, and the Nimitzes stood in that receiving line and shook hands with them all...

Q: He was about 70 then, wasn't he?

Adm. M.: At least 70. And, my goodness, when at long last my wife and I got to the Nimitzes in that receiving line, here again was the same old thing. He called us both by first names, you know. It was just fantastic, and I'm sure you've heard this from endless numbers of people that you've talked to.

Our final meeting with the Nimitzes was in either late '60 or early '61, I'm not sure - at the dedication of that new Raytheon plant in Portsmouth, near Newport, Rhode Island. Actually, people call it in Newport, but it's in the township lines of Portsmouth, I think. I was on duty in the Navy Department in the antisubmarine business. Raytheon was very important to us. I was amongst those invited to attend, and did, took Emily, my wife, up to the ceremony, and hadn't realized that Admiral Nimitz was going to be there. Charles Francis Adams was an official of the company and a former Secretary of the Navy...

Q: He was Secretary.

Mustin - 28

Adm. M.: Secretary of the Navy. We thought he was going to be the principal speaker. He was not. He introduced Admiral Nimitz, who was there.

That evening we went to a dinner party given by the Hamels - Roger Hamel, a Vice President of Raytheon who was general manager of that plant. He's still with the company, incidentally. He's here in Washington now, still with the rank of Vice President, running their Washington office, so you can see what the lobbying industry is going through. But, in any case, the Hamels had a large and lovely dinner party and included were the Nimitzes.

Of course, by this time now, roughly January '61, he was the center of not just polite attention, you know, but of avid interest. Everybody at that dinner, a wide cross section including wives, just crowded arounded to listen to the stories, anecdotes, remarks, and observations that he had to make.

Not inveighing against the "times ain't what they used to be," or "things have gone to the dogs," or "we've got to watch out for the Communists taking over," or something like that, but just amusing, pithy, and pertinent commentaries on the passing scene, or "why, I haven't seen you since we were in Manila together," or something like that, you know. Just the most voluble, outgoing flow of personal manifestations that you could ever imagine...

Q: And this was roughly at the age of 75?

Adm. M.: Yes, and by now quite hard of hearing, but just the same, that didn't diminish in any way the fact that people literally might break away from this group to accept another refill of their drink or something, but they would turn back and just listen to the conversation. Just listen.

Of course, I haven't seen him since then.

Q: You referred to the fact that he was very hard of hearing at that point. Catherine Lay said that she thought he always had a hearing defect. Is that your understanding also?

Adm. M.: I certainly had never noticed it during that time in the Augusta. Never. And I really think I perhaps said almost as much as I could about his later and more senior days that would mean anything to you, unless you have some questions. But I'd like to go back and say a little something more about those Augusta days.

Q: I would like very much to have you do so. Yes, please.

Adm. M.: This is a little bit of further recollection concerning what's known as the Operational Test and Evaluation Force. Somewhere along in late '44 or early '45, the battleship force in the Pacific had been divided into two parts. The old battleships of World War I types were called Battleship Squadron 1, and all of the new ones, all of the post World War II ones, of which the Washington and North Carolina were the first, were Battleship Squadron 2, and we called them the fast battleships.

They were the ones that had 30-knot speed and so on, to keep up with the Fleet, and Admiral Lee was the commander of the fast battleships. They were modern in every way, powerful, fast, flexible, and very useful. They stayed - when they weren't doing something particular, they stayed with the carriers, because they could keep up with them and they were very valuable radar platforms and antiaircraft gun platforms.

There were plans, and we exercised them, for peeling them off periodically to form a surface striking force interposed between ourselves and the Japanese striking force, if necessary, or for other purposes. Fragments of that force would be peeled off to go and do a bombardment job, and I had done that while still in the Miami, which operated with the carriers for a while, but got peeled off to shoot up a few islands.

The fast battleships went in and did an extensive feint, bombardment, of Okinawa before the landings. We spent a whole day bombarding in an area where we were not going to land, to deceive the Japanese defenses. Of course, this took us right in to where the Japanese, if they could have done it, could have hit us hard with aviation. Anyway, the next thing that happened was that after that was over, Admiral Lee's flagship South Dakota went back to Guam, for discussions by Admiral Lee with Admiral Nimitz' staff and headquarters concerning strike bombardments of northern Japan.

There was not a great deal, but some significant, Japanese industry in the northern parts of the country, which were beyond the strike radius of the B-29s, even using Iwo Jima. Admiral Nimitz wanted to attack that, to deprive them of the products - there were steel plants and the like - and also, as a rather somber psychological factor to the Japanese, a reminder that now the homeland was vulnerable to attack from the sea against which they had no defense.

So we spent a great deal of time and detail going through the exact structural details of these factories and planning how we were going to attack them with gunfire to accomplish the kinds of destruction that were wanted. From there we went back to join the rest of the Fleet in Leyte Gulf. And the next sortie was going to among other things, do this bombardment.

Well, at this time, came the word that Admiral Lee was going to be summoned home to found this OPDevFor. Needless to say, he received this with quite mixed emotions, because he was going to have to turn over his command to another officer whose appreciation of what was required, and how to do it right, I don't think he had the highest of confidence in...

Q: Well, the identity had been known?

Adm. M.: Oh, yes. We knew exactly who it was. When Admiral Lee was told what his new job was, and what the level of interest was, and that his assignment to it was not negotiable and so on and so forth, he picked out the people that he wished to take with him; me, and his operations officer, and his flag lieutenant. I think that was it. Three of us. This meant that the gunnery part of this bombardment had to be turned over to the gunnery officer of that new admiral. Well, Admiral Lee had known that gunnery officer professionally somewhere. I had not. He was years senior to me, but Admiral Lee characterized him as knowing a whole lot of things that weren't so. So he was quite concerned and, as it turned out, rightly so. They took a very carefully developed plan and, according to underground accounts from those who were there, just botched the execution of it beyond belief. And we were not free of that sort of thing in the Pacific war...

Q: It's the human element that's always neglected, isn't it?

Adm. M.: Yes. There really was very little excuse for this. At that point in the war, we had people who were certainly no novices. They were complete veterans, quite proficient technically and knew what to do. But we also had that rush of people out from Washington to get their Legion of Merit before it was too late, you know. The war was rather obviously getting near an end.

Q: I've heard from various sources that the frequent high-level conferences between Nimitz and King out on the Coast were largely concerned with placing senior officers who were a problem.

Adm. M.: I believe it. And this was the kind of problem to which Admiral Nimitz would, indeed, address himself personally rather than leaving it to his staff while he attended to other things. In other words, he recognized the essentiality of the individual, and the attributes of the individual as the key cogs in the machinery. No matter how marvelous a fighting machine we had there, it could be bogged down by some lack of thought in the routine assignment of people into it, into top positions. Those were the people that wound up botching this thing.

The general regard was that the most difficult operations were the carrier striking force operations. The aviators had an absolutely ironclad "go", "no go" selection process, and it didn't matter who you were, if you didn't pass screening through that process, you didn't get an aviation command in the front lines in the Pacific.

Q: Compassion didn't enter into it?

Adm. M.: Not one whit. They hadn't quite gotten that extensive a surveillance scheme, quite that ruthless a follow-through on the results of it, in other than the aviation Navy.

So, this bombardment job was botched. Well, Admiral Lee was quite uneasy that that would happen. He would never say anything like this to us junior officers, but I'm satisfied of it, and I'm satisfied that his uneasiness about this job was well known and well understood to Admiral Nimitz.

We left the South Dakota in Leyte Gulf, got aboard a PT boat, went down somewhere to where there was an alleged airfield on Samar, from which we could fly to Guam, about 1,300 miles. And the first step was to repair post haste to Admiral Nimitz' headquarters, as I mentioned, where there ensued a lot of discussions, the principal ones between

Admiral Nimitz and Admiral Lee, on just what was this new assignment that had led to Admiral Lee's being uprooted out of his command and sent back to the States.

And, of course, here we learned that Admiral Nimitz knew exactly what it was, and felt that it was urgent that the job be done.

I am not actually sure who should properly be credited with the idea of putting together a group for the purpose that OpDevFor was formed for, a group formed for that purpose and staffed by people of that kind. It used to be loosely said that it was Admiral King's idea, but I always felt after that time there - and my recollection is that we spent more than a day there on Guam in this kind of discussion - I've always felt that Admiral Nimitz had a hand in it. In looking at what lay ahead in the invasion of Japan, he'd constantly been made aware in general of what all the marvelous products were in laboratories back here, and I suspect it was he who raised the question, that none of that is going to do us any good unless we not only have it, but have it in operational quantity. A new radar must not just be on the books in Washington, it's got to be mounted on the ships that are there when the landing forces go ashore, and its going to take strong decisons to get them there.

Q: You didn't want to be dealing with prototypes. You wanted the whole thing.

Adm. M.: He wanted his force equipped, and he had to do something about deciding where to place the emphasis in order to get it equipped, and the man who could do that was Lee. Now, this could be known to King, but King had other things on his mind. I'm satisfied that the only person in a position to control these things, who could have really known how acute the problem was, how disappointed we had been in some Washington products - King wouldn't know that back here in Washington, except indirectly - the only person in a position to control these things, who could have really known how acute the problem was, how disappointed we had been in some Washington products - King wouldn't know that back here in Washington, except indirectly - the only person who would know that, and the only person who could reliably put the finger on the man for the job of sorting out the good from the bad, and the timely from the untimely, in time for that invasion of Japan must necessarily have been Nimitz.

I've always felt that regardless of what the record shows, the idea came from him, by word of mouth, if nothing else. He and his senior staff spent a lot of time outlining their concern, the feeling that we needed certain new things that the state of the art ought to offer, but where is it, you know, how come we can't get it, and this sort of thing.

Q: I wonder if I could possibly substantiate this through the recollections of some staff member who's still extant. Would Mercer have any idea?

Adm. M.: I'm not sure.

Q: Would Layton have any idea?

Adm. M.: The fellow who would know more likely than any other, I believe, would be Tom Hill - T. B. Hill, who was Nimitz' Fleet gunnery officer etc. and was concerned with the center of gravity of this thought, which was in the weapons or counter-weapons area - the radar and gunnery and so forth area. And I would expect Admiral Hill to be quite likely to be more knowledgeable than almost any other single individual. Mercer was the flag secretary, so he - it is possible that he would know, but I wouldn't be surprised if not, because it might have been purely on a personal basis, and the key phases of the whole idea handled that way had then made known into the action channels, which would be Tom Hill. Fitzhugh Lee, who's around...

Q: He's out on the Coast.

Adm. M.: He's living in Coronado. Fitz Lee, incidentally, was one of our old Augusta shipmates. Fitz was on Admiral Nimitz' staff at that time, but I think he was his PIO, which seemed an odd assignment for Fitz, really, and may not related very closely to knowledge of this.

In any case, we left Guam eastbound to start OpDevFor with a very clearly developed idea, first of all, of what Admiral Nimitz felt was needed and the urgency with which he felt that way, and, secondly, some pretty strong ideas of his and of his staff's, and of our own, of what we had to do in order for it to have any meaning. Not only did the things we were to test have to seem like good ideas, but they had to be far enough along so that emergency priorities could lead to things being produced and delivered and installed, wired up or whatever you have, in quantities sufficient to make a difference in the conduct of the fighting.

Admiral Lee was very open, in that small staff that he had, with even the most private communications, if they bore on official actions. I don't recall the specifics, but I have a vague recollection that he had heard some inklings of the new job by message before we left the flagship in Leyte. But it wasn't until this time that we spent on Guam that he really had the picture of what the problem was, and how-seriously it was regarded at Admiral Nimitz' level.

Q: Did he then begin to show some enthusiasm for the new assignment?

Adm. M.: I'll have to put that negatively. His disappointment at leaving his command seemed to be far less manifest, if you can call that some enthusiasm. He was just a wonderful man. He was a thorough professional.

Q: He wanted to see the war to the end?

Adm. M.: That's right, and he felt that there were things to be done that he understood, and ways of doing them that he understood, and interrelationships with the other commanders out there that he understood. He and Pete Mitscher were dearest friends. They understood each other completely, and he knew he could work in that environment and he was quite disappointed at having to leave it. But he certainly left Guam eastbound with a very strong appreciation of what had to be done, and how he had to do it. And, in fact, before he left Guam, he originated some actions to get certain selected other people moved into this business with him. So, there can't be any question but what the encounters there, and this was June of '45, conveyed to Admiral Lee, for his guidance in setting up this OpDevFor business, a pretty complete picture of just what Admiral Nimitz expected of it, hoped for from it, felt a very pressing need for from it.

Q: Another question that comes to mind, when you once got to Washington and began working with this area, did you meet with enthusiasm on the part of Admiral Hussey?

Adm. M.: This, of course, is quite pertinent to the whole thing and, I suppose, to the whole story, and one that I also ought to answer in a mixed way. I really don't have very strong feelings on it.

Our first contacts, of course, were with Admiral King, briefly on Admiral Lee's part. Then his immediate senior staff, and quickly down to Arleigh Burke's level, where the question was, we know what we're going to do, now we want to talk about the details of how we do it.

Admiral Hussey and Admiral Lee had known each other well for years, and I'm sure each respected the other extensively, but Admiral Lee had needled Admiral Hussey rather strongly on this VT fuze business that I described. Admiral Hussey had been here in Washington running the Bureau of Ordnance as best he could, and he didn't know anything about that, you know, but here was one of his products being held up to fairly strong criticism, and several other of his products were too. And Lee, who knew his stuff, was always the focal point of this well-directed criticism.

He was the origin of it, let us say. He was at the origin of it. So there could have been a few reservations there.

I don't honestly believe, though, that they were material. I think the situation there was one that really rather readily lent itself to just being played straight. Hussey would say, "Here's what we've got, several items obviously of a nature to compete each with the other, you pick out the one you want. Here's then what we might be able to do about putting all our resources into producing that one in quantities you can use."

Relationships were just a little bit more strained with the Bureau of Ships and, of course, that MTI radar was one of their darlings and when we gave that a rather brutal down check, the tension rose in Washington. But Arleigh Burke fended all that off down at this end, and Charley Martell was in Arleigh Burke's office and he's a very able operator in the Washington environment and did awfully well.

In any case, once we got going in OpDevFor, then we simply undertook to do the best we could, based on what we had brought back from the Pacific with us, but there were no further particular contacts with Admiral Nimitz because, of course, the war ended in August.

Well, I said I'd like to talk a little bit...

Q: To focus on the Augusta.

Adm. M.: ...about the Augusta days and I mentioned to you that when Admiral Nimitz came to her as the new commanding officer, there was a situation that in today's terms would have to be recognized as little short of chaotic.

The ship was in the Navy Yard, undergoing a delayed overhaul conducted at the wrong time for the wrong reasons, going out to the China station where there really was no proper Navy Yard capability, nevertheless having to put up with a bobtailed overhaul, with an almost hundred percent turnover of the crew, a hundred percent turnover of all the officers except six ensigns, nothing like shakedown or refresher training after the overhaul, and, heavens, the third captain in three months or something like that.

Well, I suppose we were all very professional. Although we ensigns were ensigns, we were now ensigns with seventeen months of experience - that's a lot of experience...

Q: You were all friends, too, which is another factor.

Adm. M.: A very closely knit group. Most, though not all, of the newly assigned officers, turned out to be real star performers. Red Whiting became an admiral, too. We set about putting that ship back together and, by present standards, things proceeded in an unusual way. The ship finished up its three-month overhaul in two months, hastily loaded stores, and sailed for China in October '33. There was no so-called refresher training or anything like it. We just got under way and went, with the majority of officers who'd never been at sea a day in that ship. Most of them, of course, had come from shore duty, indeed.

Well, it bespeaks a lot for the basic professional quality of the officer corps of the day, that you could do things like that, but it also tells you a great deal about Captain Nimitz' professional qualities and leadership that we could do it.

We steamed across the Pacific direct, Great Circle route, as close as you can take one, from Seattle to Shanghai. We went up the river, moored in the Wanpoo at Shanghai where the Houston was, and prepared to receive on board the staff of Commander-in-Chief, Asiatic Fleet, a four-star admiral...

Q: That was Admiral Upham.

Adm. M.: It was Admiral Upham...and get on with the job of being the flagship of the fleet.

Just incidentally, a great deal of attention was paid in those days to the so-called gunnery year training cycle. It was done on a very highly formalized basis. Typically, it began in the late summer and early fall and went on into the late fall each year. Ours had been prevented by our peculiar schedule on the West Coast, so when we finally arrived down in Manila in about December '33 we had a whole gunnery year still to do, and as soon as we got finished with it, then we had to do next year's gunnery year because, as the Fleet flagship, we were going to have to go off somewhere else where we couldn't get the necessary target services and the like to do it.

So in what was going to be three or four months in Manila, we had to do two gunnery years back to back. Well, the ship simply went through all of these things under Captain Nimitz' leadership, and it was there. It was manifest in everything that went on from day to day. It was manifest in every way he had of doing business, and I suppose even then, as ensigns, we could see that the man left nothing to chance that could be handled better if properly prepared for.

Just navigating that ship around in those China station waters, for instance. Amongst other things, I found myself the assistant navigator. The navigator was an officer with a lot of background in intelligence. It was thought important, I guess, to have such a capability on board, but he'd never done any navigation. Well, the only navigation I'd ever done was what I'd been taught to do at the Naval Academy...

Q: But you were a star there in that area, weren't you?

Adm. M.: Well...

Q: Didn't you come out No. 1...

Adm. M.: Oh, I don't think so. But anyway, it turned out that the navigator couldn't navigate. Somehow - eye peculiarity or something -- he couldn't take a star sight or a sun sight. So the quartermaster and I took all the celestial sights and did all of that part of the navigation.

Well, Admiral Nimitz had that navigation bridge very carefully organized so that not only were we - when we were on soundings, as the seamen say, when we were doing piloting, the plotted track of where we were was not only very meticulously kept, but it was kept on a basis that was visible to him any time he wished to walk over there and see how the navigation was going. And there was nothing slipshod about it. The things you read about in collisions and groundings and so forth were unknown on that bridge. They just did not happen.

Many of the places that we went were very poorly charted. For example, the first time we went into Tsingtao Harbor the charts were based on surveys dated about 1845. A navigator's reliability test for his navigational landmarks is to get cross bearings on a number of them and plot them on the chart, and they should all intersect in a point. Well, you never got points out of that Tsingtao chart. So, the next thing you know, I'm ashore in Tsingtao making contact with Chinese maritime authorities to get copies of their charts, which we did, and although the characters were all Chinese on them, that was all right, we recongized the things, and they were very good. They were meticulous, with cross bearings with lots of points etc., so only then was Captain Nimitz satisfied with the basic ability to navigate that ship in and out of Tsingtao Harbor.

Needless to say, this chart was duly packaged up, copies of it, and sent back to Washington for improving our charts. Wherever we went, information of this kind was gathered not only for his own use, but it was also put into the stream to go back to the improvement of the system.

Q: He was, in fact, his own intelligence officer.

Adm. M.: Yes, and in a much broader sense, really, than intelligence is often visualized. But this meticulous care in the navigation of that ship was perhaps what struck us first, because in those days the China coast was poorly charted, as I've just described. It was poorly marked by navigational aids, also, lighthouses. There were many of them, but many on that long coast was not very many per unit distance, you know, and there were things that changed and were almost unchartable, like in that great estuary of the Yangtze River, tremendous volumes of sediment coming down were changing the channel configurations all the time, naturally, and it was really a problem.

We were never in trouble because whatever we were going to do, it was always looked at ahead of time. If you had to write a text book for the guidance of a young commanding officer on how to keep yourself out of trouble by looking ahead, being foresighted, and making your plans and preparations accordingly, this was it. It was the perfect display of this, and it showed immediately upon getting there, to my eyes, because I was the assistant navigator and this was where it showed.

It began showing in other things, too. The gunnery exercises that we had to fire were all very carefully laid out as to what you would do, and how many shots you should fire, and all of that, and how you should score these shots, and that was all there in the rules, so you could - reading the rules, you could see what am I supposed to do next, and I fully ready to do that, yes, no. If not, let us complete those preparations.

And the results began to show. We fired the same gunnery practices as everybody else, by the same rules, and they were scored just as rigorously, if not slightly more so for a reason I'll mention in a minute. But we began making higher scores than anybody else was making. Not just in the Asiatic Fleet, in the entire U.S. Navy, They were all fired out of one rule book, and the records were all compared against everybody else.

And so, not surprisingly, when we wound up in our first full competitive year under Captain Nimitz, we won the battle efficiency trophy. There was one for cruisers, that's all. There wasn't one in every squadron or something, like it has been later; there was one, and we had it, and we had it by a mile. There were no close seconds.

And why did we have it by a mile? Well, we went out one night to fire one of the prescribed practices, night battle practice. We had some people, including Captain Nimitz, who thought this fighting with modern gunnery in the daytime can be too lethal. The weak side is going to want to seek engagements at night, and that may be us, or it may be the other guy, but we want to win, so let's pay attention to this.

What can we do, what are our problems, what are our limitations? And we had some pretty good schemes for doing better at night, and when the scores were all added up, it turned out that the Augusta's score on that night battle practice was slightly larger than the sum of the scores of the next three highest cruisers in the U.S. Navy. That's why we won the battle efficiency medal, because that's the kind of shooting we did. You don't win at shooting without meticulous and careful and laborious and painstaking preparation, and we had it.

Q: As a bit of a digression, isn't it unfortunate that this technique that you began to develop for night fighting was not more widespread in the Fleet when we came to encounters with the Japanese?

Mustin - 46

Adm. M.: Yes, and I'll tell you, when I was out there in the Pacific as a gunnery officer in a cruiser during the war, those techniques were "prevalent" in my ship. And I used to talk to all of my friends and colleagues and contemporaries, do my best by word of mouth to explain to them some of these things.

The extent to which they ever got into written, doctrinal-type publications, I just don't know, and I fear it was not very extensive, because to allude to a punch line from an old prewar Benchley story, the governing consideration in some of those Navy tactical and doctrinal books seemed to be, don't get it right, get it written.

Some of them were pretty bad. Some of them preached as doctrine things that are just wrong, and all you could do about this officially was write it all down on paper with your explanation of why, and then this was cranked into the mill. This was one man's opinion, and it was weighed equally against 400 other guys who had never heard a shot fired in anger, and the weighted average came out, probably. A pretty futile business.

But in any case, what Augusta gunnery showed was Nimitz' characteristics.

There was an athletic competition out there in the Asiatic Fleet, fleetwide. The Fleet rules on this were quite explicit. They said, in effect, that living out here in this kind of climate and under these conditions, special measures are necessary for the physical well-being of the ships' companies, and therefore participation in the Fleet athletic program is mandatory, that is to say, it is required that when there is going to be a baseball competition, you field a baseball team. You be there. Furthermore, it is mandatory that practice times for all these teams be provided during normal working hours, rather than having them in the men's liberty time. So, it was pretty obvious that athletics were taken quite seriously in the Asiatic Fleet.

Of course, Admiral Nimitz was a very physically vigorous, alert sort of man himself all the years that I knew him, and this was not a hardship to him to have to do this. He thought this was just about right, and that's the way he wanted his ship's company to be, and OK, they say we're going to have to have a team in this competition, let's go. Let's get up the team.

One of the sports was rugby, of all things. They played it out there because you could always get competition with the British. Needless to say, we didn't have anybody who'd ever played rugby, but we got up a team and, in fact, Muddy Waters coached it. The next thing you know, we had the Fleet rugby trophy.

We had to build a new trophy case because by the time we wound up we had them all, every Fleet athletic trophy there was, tennis, everything without exception. One by one, we took them away from the Canopus, which was a submarine tender. As a tender she spent most of her time in port. Submarines would come alongside and get tended, and they culled all the good athletes out of the submarines and assigned them to the tender, and for years out there they'd had all the best teams in everything.

When the Augusta began winning the trophies, typically most of them we gained by subtraction from the Canopus, and feelings got more and more intense. In the summers we went to Tsingtao and operated mostly out of there, and so did the Canopus. So, the rivalry was a very intimate one.

Well, we hadn't been out there very long, and we were well down this road toward separating them from all their long-held and deeply cherished athletic trophies, when some legislation was passed back home to provide what we knew as "exchange relief." Just about the time that we went out there, the dollar was devalued, as you may remember, and this was a tremendous financial hardship because the prices on the local economy did not go down, and our total pay really went down to about 60 or 70 percent of what it had been in real value in the local economy, and we all lived on the economy. There wasn't any other way of living. So some legislation was passed to provide for this - the exchange relief, and lo, it was made retroactive and effective as of a certain day. Everybody got paid an additional amount in dollars so that they would have a total dollar take equivalent in local purchasing power to what they had before devaluation. We all got back pay on this, so everybody had big fat bundles of back pay in hand, and it was about 40 percent of your total of both pay and allowances. Everybody had many months of this retroactive back pay in hand at the time of the big finals in the whale boat race, and we took the whale boat trophy and all the money away from the Canopus. Well, again, this athletic competition was a manifestation of the way he went at things.

Q: Does this spring from his Germanic background, do you think, in part?

Adm. M.: I wouldn't have thought so, really, although there was a certain teutonic thoroughness about him, but not that plodding, pedantic thoroughness, just an alert, forehanded thoroughness, and there's a difference, perhaps vague, but there is one, to my way of thinking.

And the reason I mention this Canopus thing was that since they were in Tsingtao and we were in Tsingtao, and most of our gunnery year was fired out of Tsingtao, the staff had to look around and find somebody to be the official referees for all those gunnery exercises, and the Canopus people whose money we were taking, and whose trophies we were taking and so forth, and whose sailors our sailors were jeering at in the White Russian cabarets ashore, were the guys who were scoring our practices. So, you can imagine that we didn't get given very much.

Q: No. It had to be obvious.

Adm. M.: We didn't get an inch. But I'll have to tell you another sea story from that time, and it was another night battle practice, the following year. One of the submarine division commanders was the chief umpire.

The way the practice was arranged, the target would be going along here and you'd come in on one leg and you'd fire with the main battery controlled by the forward main battery control station, spot one, and so forth. The target would be completely dark, you see, and there'd be some clue - we didn't have radar, of course - some clue would reveal it, like the flash of some searchlight or something, and you'd have to then fire a spread of star shells out there to find it and illuminate it, fire on it with the main battery, turn and come back the other way, the target would be revealed again, and you had to illuminate it with searchlights, fire on it with the main battery controlled from the after group, spot two, and then you'd come in on a third leg and fire at it with the 5-inch.

And when this was all over, the sea was pretty rough, you couldn't get aboard the target that night. We towed the target into port. The next morning a boat from the Canopus came over and picked up a couple of us ensigns to go and assist the observing party in recording the hits on target. You fired at a so-called battle raft, and you scored the hits by actual physical hits, in its 140-foot long, 40-foot high target screen of wooden battens, supported on a raft made of heavy timbers.

Well, when we'd gotten around to the inner harbor where the tug had moored this raft, and we came up to it in the motor boat, here was a horrible sight. The screen was just a shambles. It was literally shot away in large areas. The shells were always painted with distinctive colors to identify hits, and in passing through these wooden screens they'd leave paint. So the official referee simply said, "Well, all right, there are a lot of holes here. Let's get started and count the paint." So we just all scrambled over the screen, you know, and one guy from the ship and one guy from the observing party; Yes, here's green paint, here, and it would be marked down, one green paint...

Q: Just like a polling booth with representatives of both parties.

Adm. M.: Yes, both sides. Well, we scrambled over this screen, did the best we could, counted all the paint, and got down in the boat again and here was the submarine officer who was the chief umpire. Being a submariner, you know, he knew what the rule book said, and he was going to do a proper job up here, but he wasn't intimately familiar with some of the details of the target practice. So when he added all the hits up, and he added up all the 8-inch hits, and he added up all the 5-inch hits, and here there emerged a very peculiar thing. He had more hits scored than we had fired shots.

So we all agreed that that wouldn't do, and some means would have to be taken to adjust his numbers downward.

What had happened was that, of course, these night battle practices were at relatively close range; an 8-inch gun had a very flat trajectory and they were coming in at low angles; any that hit short would ricochet and go through the screen, many of them had hit right in the raft itself, and that was a valid hit, of course, but an 8-inch inert shell plunging into a nest of timbers just erupts a fountain of splinters up through this screen and takes out whole sections of it. The projectiles had windshields on the ogives, but these windshields would come off on water impact and the windshield would go through with paint on it and the shell itself would go through with paint on it, and the screen was so shot up you couldn't see whether or not it was a nice clean round hole, and one way or another, we had more hits scored than we'd fired shots.

So the referee said, "Well - the tug had been there, of course, observing this thing, doing what they called raking the shot, the rake being the thing that looks sort of like a rake with the tines upward, and you looked through it, you know, center it up on the tug and then you could observe against these tines how far over or short the various splashes were. Not a very precise, but approximate way of confirming where the shots were. It was agreed by negotiation that any shots identified by the rakes that were recorded far enough away from the target that they could not possibly have hit it, they would be judged as misses. So, we began by subtracting all the provable misses from these totals, and the net was the hits we were credited with, and, of course, again, there wasn't anybody in the Navy that had a score that remotely approached the Augusta's.

Well, I think there is another area of, you might say, competitive evaluation, and it still survives in the Navy today. In that time it was called Admiral's Inspection, and it was the big inspection that the ship got, roughly once a year.

Today they call them administrative inspections and they have mile-long checkoff lists and so forth, but the general philosophy is the same. The intensity of detailed scrutiny of everything is more or less the same, that is, internal procedures, record-keeping, accounts, pay accounts, other kinds of accounts, files, the cleanliness of the ship, the meticulousness with which the damage control checkoff lists were up to date and accurate, and all of that. The crew, of course, is inspected at quarters meticulously, and the berthing spaces and the machinery spaces, and everything are gone over with a fine-tooth comb.

A mark of outstanding on one of these inspections is rare, indeed, and it is so rare that, typically, a mark of outstanding on an inspection like this was, and still is, the basis for a special letter of commendation to the commanding officer.

Well, unfortunately for the Augusta, what with one thing and another, including a cruise we made from Chinwantao to Australia and all the way around Australia and up through the Indies and the Southern Philippines, this Admiral's Inspection, which was supposed to be completed before the end of the year, hadn't been done when we got in to Manila on something like the 20th of December, from a 12,000 or 15,000-mile cruise. So the inspection was scheduled to be held on the 22nd of December. And the long and short of it was that we got an "outstanding" on it...

Q: Had the Admiral been with you on the cruise to Australia?

Adm. M.: He had been aboard the ship, but this was still Stumpy Upham, as we called him...

Q: Stumpy?

Adm. M.: A little short fellow. A wonderful guy, and a marvelous naval officer. But he had no particular illusions about one ship over another, and the inspection was going to be done to his standards or else. The assistant inspectors, of course, were again our friends from the Canopus, so if they could find a speck of dirt, they found it.

But you'd go down in the engine rooms and everything was bright work. The floor plates were bright work, not just clean or well painted, they were bright work. Well, they were aluminum, those were treaty cruisers, so this was aluminum bright work floor plates. The interconnecting piping down in the bilge, under the floor plates, say lubricating oil piping from the sumps under the turbine reduction gears into the oil cooler, and thence back to be recirculated through the engine, typically that kind of piping was, and still is, copper. The copper was bright work, like your wife's pans hanging in the kitchen, not just clean copper, but bright work, shined with brass polish, like the bottoms of those pans there.

Why was that? Well, that was simply because there wasn't a sailor in that ship who wasn't going to have his little nook or cranny or corner, not only spotless, but better than anybody else's nook or cranny or corner had ever been, because that's the way they wanted it for their captain. And that was the spirit that permeated that ship.

It had some humorous aspects in a way, not bad by the standards of the day. When we'd be in Shanghai, moored bow and stern to buoys in the Wangpoo, there were a lot of electroplating shops ashore, chrome plate. The Chinamen polished everything up for you with mechanical machine buffers and so on, and then chrome plated it for you, for very little money. So holy smoke, the turret crews would just, piece by piece, dismount items out of their turrets, take 'em ashore, have them back, and install 'em, and pay for it out of their own pockets.

Q: Unbeknownst to the captain?

Adm. M.: Unbeknownst to anybody. Paid for out of their own pockets. Of course, if while the cover off some turret ready light switch was ashore being chrome plated, you'd had to do any fighting, why, you couldn't activate that turret. But we didn't live in a constant climate of having to be ready to shoot ten minutes from now in those days and, lo and behold, you wound up with chrome plated turret insides, and things like that.

That was just the way the sailors responded to the over-all leadership in that ship, which was imparted by the captain, through the command pyramid of his officers, and, obviously, of course, from the officers through the men.

I think Captain Nimitz' tour in command of that ship, where nothing that he did could possibly ever be far from the scrutiny of a four-star admiral, was a very meaningful test and trial of his capabilities. If he'd had any shortcomings, they couldn't have gone unnoticed. At the same time, if he had abilities to do better than average, this too wouldn't go unnoticed, and obviously it did not.

You know, one thing he believed in very strongly was that the junior officers should handle that ship...

Q: Yes, do tell me about that time he took to train you.

Adm. M.: Well, he did it. For example, I was in the first division for a while, and we were coming in to a perfectly unknown place, Tutu Bay, down in the southern Philippines. I was just an ensign, and a lieutenant was the division officer, and you can't imagine how senior a lieutenant was, he was so senior that I still think of him as being pretty senior, in fact. A messenger came down from the bridge and said Lieutenant Dahlgren is wanted on the bridge. So Joe Dahlgren started expostulating about bringing the ship to anchor and turning the forecastle over to Ensign Mustin etc.

Well, I'd been there in the first division for a few weeks or a month, I suppose I should have known how to bring the ship to anchor, Well, Captain Nimitz wasn't going to leave it to theory. He sent for Joe Dahlgren to come up to the bridge, and said, "Now, Joe, I just want you here because I don't want you down on the forecastle. I want to see if a junior officer can handle the forecastle." So, he did. Well, you could botch up an anchoring, you could even maim people, kill 'em, in mishandling that kind of gear, anchoring in deep water, a good problem. Captain Nimitz did it.

That was the first time that happened there. Every other ensign in the ship got the word, so they made damned sure that they were ready for the artificial removal of their boss, to do their boss' job with the old man looking down from the bridge.

When you had the watch on the bridge, he'd do the same thing. Holy smoke, this was in 1933 or 1934 - Joe Dahlgren was in the class of '24 at the Naval Academy. Ten years' experience. Oh, my, he was older than God to us ensigns.

Q: There was a generation gap, too.

Adm. M.: Yes. Well, he'd take the officer of the deck, he'd say, "Lieutenant Dahlgren, come here a moment please. Turn the conn over to the junior officer of the deck," and you'd have to handle the ship, bring her to anchor, or take her through a channel, or what have you. Well, if something had gone wrong, it might have endangered the ship, although I personally don't believe that any longer.

Q: It might have endangered the reputation of the captain.

Adm. M.: It could have made the ship look a little bad, as the flagship of a four-star admiral. Well, he believed so strongly in bringing up his junior officers to where they could do these things, that he never let how he looked to the admiral interfere with what he felt he should do for those ensigns, and he let them handle the ship. This is a lesson that's well understood by any naval officer who's ever had command of a ship.

Q: Is it a general practice?

Adm. M.: I'm afraid it's not. I wish it were. It's one of the things that I've personally tried to stress. Of course, ever since then, I could only go one way in my own personal views. I was at sea all through the war and I've been at sea through other emergency situations, and I have come to feel something pretty strongly which I don't think I've ever heard articulated, certainly not in things like seamanship instruction books at the Naval Academy and so on, and that is that the ship is not in its strongest position, the ship doesn't have its best chance to do its best, if the captain has to preoccupy himself with conning the ship. Conning the ship is ensigns' work. The captain can tell the ensign, now put her alongside that tanker, or, now take her through there, or, now bring her around broadside so the whole gun battery can bear over there, but then he's got to be free to think of other things. Conning is a moment-to-moment detailed thing, and you are a hundred percent preoccupied with it when you're doing it, and your attention is preempted from other things that the captain should attend to, the bigger picture.

Q: This is the art of delegating authority.

Adm. M.: Well, it's a very necessary art in my opinion. When I had a destroyer squadron, I had some captains who insisted on taking the conn themselves whenever any special maneuver was to be done, and I simply told hem, you're derelict in your responsibilities for the combat readiness of your ship if you follow this procedure. If you don't have officers who can conn and leave you free to fight the ship, your ship is not ready, and I'm going to mark you down accordingly. And you're derelict in your responsibilities to the seamanship capabilities of the ship, and you're derelict in your responsibilities for training your officers. And I made them believe it.

When I had a destroyer flotilla, I told my squadron commanders these thoughts, and I told them any time any of their captains ever got into trouble, which I didn't think they would, when it seemed to be related to the fact that the officer of the deck was conning the ship, I was not going to admit of any disposition of the situation on the basis that obviously the captain wasn't at the conn and he should have been. The answer is the captain was not at the conn and the captain should not have been at the conn, so what really caused the trouble? Find out.

And when I was in command of the Amphibious Force, I was in a pretty final position relative to the captains then, and I just told them, "This is what you've got to do. If you don't do it, you're not satisfactory, If you do do it, I'm going to back you. I'm telling you, I'm directing you, and requiring you to do it. Go do it and I'll back you."

But this is one person's view, and there are so many others who don't share it, unfortunately. I don't know how many of them would survive. When I had command of a destroyer, I relieved a captain who had only three officers in that ship who he permitted to stand officer of the deck watch. He didn't allow anybody else on the bridge, except the officer on watch. When the simplest evolution had to be done, he took the conn himself and did it, not very well either, and there may be some correlation there...

Q: You have to be master of a technique yourself before you can delegate it.

Adm. M.: Perhaps. I took command of the ship just about the time she was going in the Navy Yard, and when we came out of the Navy Yard only one of those three officers was left. I didn't have any others that had ever been on the bridge of that destroyer under way. We had to start fast, so I just said from now on every line officer in this ship stands officer of the deck watches. He rotates. Stands watch down below in CIC and rotates back up to the deck daily. And whoever's watch it is in the normal rotation does whatever has to be done. If the ship's in port and it's time to get under way, he gets it under way. He gets clear of the mess. He gets clear of the buoy or what-have-you. If we're coming back to port at the end of the week, he picks up the buoy or he gets alongside the nest. Re-fuel at sea, he does it.

Well, I came to realize, in trying to put all these pieces together, tracing all the way back to Captain Nimitz, not only did he teach his people things which they were eager to learn and very well able to learn, but having taught them, he put himself in a position where, when he had to divert his attention to something else, he was able to do it because the officer with the conn could do what he wanted him to do. And he knew it. He didn't just have it as a theory. He knew it because he'd given himself the opportunity to observe it over a long period.

As a ship's captain, I found myself with a rescue at sea on my hands in rough seas. This was the Piedmont, a big ship. I couldn't see being in the pilot house conning the ship. I was out on the bridge wing, gravely concerned about getting the whale boat back without killing people, and things like that.

But in addition to what it does for the officer's personal capabilities and feelings, think of the difference it makes to all the men in his division. Why should I look up to this fellow who's my division officer? When he's got the watch on the bridge, anytime anything is to happen, the old man takes the conn away from him, won't let him do it. On the other hand, when their division officers are up there running things, whether they like it or not the men subconsciously recognize a feeling of respect, and it just spreads.

When I had command of that destroyer, in that division three other captains were the kind that took the conn every time. Money couldn't buy the feelings that my officers had relative to their officers, because when you bring a destroyer alongside the nest, the conning officer on the bridge can call across to the far bridge in the nest, it's just that close. Everybody on every bridge on every destroyer sees who's at the conn. And while the captains of the other destroyers were doing it, my ensigns were doing it. So we won the battle efficiency pennant and they didn't. There isn't any doubt in my mind that this was a factor.

And it was a factor there when Captain Nimitz had command of the Augusta, I am satisfied.

Q: You supply, Admiral, a missing bit of information to something that Chester Jr. told me about his father's technique in expecting officers to measure up and, very often, without specific instructions to them. Just simply expecting them to measure up to a certain set of circumstances. It puzzled me a bit, but now I understand, because he never expected them to measure up unless he knew they could do it.

Adm. M.: Or, if they couldn't, it was high time to find it out, and he had a few that he thought didn't measure up and he was quite unequivocal about getting rid of them, under conditions that caused this to reflect appropriately in their records, and in due course, the Navy system got rid of them.

Q: This leads me to a question about the judgments rendered by the captain for infractions of rules and so forth. The captain's mast, would you talk about that on the Augusta?

Adm. M.: Well, that's something I have almost no memories about, which in itself is a good sign because I was in the ship for four years. Two of those four were under Captain Nimitz. We had the invarying policy in that ship the whole time I was in it that if a man was hailed before the captain at mast, why, his division officer was there too, to speak for the man or about the man, and partly just to let the officer know that there was a question of how come this malefactor has come out of your division? What's the matter with you, that your guys are doing things wrong? Now this, too, is a little bit of...

Q: Brother's keeper idea?

Adm. M.: Well, damn it, you know Navy regs used to say and may still say, when you turn over to that chapter that talks about the duties and responsibilities and so forth of a division officer, it starts off by telling you what a division officer is, and it says a division officer is an officer who commands a division. The wise framers of those rules long ago recognized that assignment as a division officer was the potential first step on the ladder of understanding the art of command in the Navy. Well, if a guy can command, you might as well hold him responsible. He's supposed to guide his men, and exert the kind of leadership such that they don't have these infractions.

I think one can safely say that the Augusta had absolutely unheard-of level of high morale, high pride and competence at every level, down to the lowest mess cook, and therefore disciplinary problems you would expect to be in a very, very small minority of your personal administrative matters with your crew. Yes, we had 'em. We had courtsmartial, you know, which meant prosecutor. Also take their turn at being somebody's defense counsel. It was not a burden. There just were not many of these. It's one of the things I have to stop to think twice to even remember that it occurred at all.

Q: Very interesting observation. Now, let us bring something else to mind. The Augusta was, in fact, the home for the great bulk of the crew, officer and men, was it not, because most of the men - and you were an exception, so was the Captain - most of the men were unmarried on this cruise.

Adm. M.: That's true. Among the officers, I suppose that of the senior officers, the lieutenants and up, they were 100 percent married. Well, in fact, when we went out to China, the class of '24, ten years out of the Naval Academy, were still JGs, and I believe all of them on up were married. But I was the only married ensign. Among the crew, in those days in the Navy, the proportion of enlisted men who were married was very small. And of those who went to China, almost zero. I think - I don't remember knowing affirmatively of a single enlisted man who took his wife to China with him. All of the married officers did.

Q: The fact that you had your wife there - did this involve you more heavily in social life on shore when you were at Tsingtao and places like that?

Adm. M.: In a way, but not what you'd really call social life. Because I was married we had a little place to live ashore. That turned out to be, as you'd expect, the headquarters ashore for all the bachelors. They were always around there. Pretty hard to call that social. They were just there.

Q: But there was an interchange of sociability between fleets, was there not? The French and the British and...

Adm. M.: Especially strong with the British. We had a very close relationship with them, that extended all the way downward from the captains, the execs, through the wardrooms. It was very active interchange of the old convention of wardroom calls, ship to ship, plus activities ashore - combined activities ashore, golf, tennis, social functions of one kind, cocktail parties and so on.

I think there's one other thing that Captain Nimitz arranged in the Augusta that you may have heard of, that ought to be on the record. When we got out to China in November '33, our point of arrival was Shanghai, and that's where we relieved the Houston of the flag. Then we went on down to Amoy, Hong Kong, and eventually Manila. We arrived down in Manila in December, and we probably left there in March, and went on up and arrived again in the spring in Shanghai. Now it appeared that the ship was going to be there for two or three months. I think the Admiral was going to disembark in a little alternate flagship, an ex-yacht, the Isabel, which was in commission as a gunboat, and go up the river to Hangkow and beyond in the Isabel, leaving the Augusta in Shanghai where he would rejoin her. So, we were going to be there in port for a while.

Captain Nimitz arranged what I would describe as a series of seminars - that's not perhaps too good a term. As I recall it, these occurred perhaps once a week. All of the officers would be assembled in the wardroom, and they'd be given a discussion about something concerning China. The first one of these was given by a Marine officer, who was the Intelligence Officer of the 4th Marine Regiment, which was the Marine regiment on duty in Shanghai, and this was about this fellow's third tour in China. He spoke the language, read the Chinese-language newspapers and so on, knew the country quite well, relatively speaking. He gave us, in about an hour's presentation, a very sketchy outline of the various things that seemed important about China as it was at that time. A little bit of its past history to explain its present situation, and so on, and he gave us all of this in the language of a fellow professional military man, so that it was in our own language. This was then followed by a succession by truly distinguished people. For example, Mr. Johnson was our Consul General out there...

Q: Nelson Johnson?

Adm. M.: Nelson Johnson, who was later our first ambassador. He had been in China, at that time, about 30 years. He spoke the language, travelled all over the country...

Q: He was the outstanding American authority...

Adm. M.: I think so, and he told us many things of what he knew and thought he knew and judged to be true about China, and he was also quite frank in outlining the many things that in 30 years there he hadn't been able to satisfy himself that he understood about it. Julian Arnold was out there. He was our commercial attaché, so-called, in those days. Julian Arnold knew all about the economy of that country, from dried eggs to who knows what. What their exports were, what their imports were, where, when, why and how, where they came from, what it meant, to this, that and the other peasant, and what was being done about everything. The Minister of Education of the Republic of China stood there in the wardroom of the Augusta and explained to us the status of education, the government's appreciation of the problems, what it was trying to do about it, how it was trying to do these things, and so on. And, incidentally, explained all these things in a kind and quality of English that you could be jealous of. He was...

Q: I don't think you could. I don't think you need be.

Adm. M.: Oh, yes. He was educated in the U.S. and of course his was one of those really profound ancient Chinese intellects. And it was just fascinating. The Minister of Finance of the Republic of China told us all about the financial situation, the monetary situation. What they were trying to - they had the most ridiculous money in that country in those days. We all lived with it. We knew it. When you left Shanghai, wherever you were going next, Shanghai money was no good there. You couldn't spend Shanghai money in Tsingtao or Amoy. You could go ashore in Amoy for an afternoon's walk, which Captain Nimitz used to like to do, walk out into the country to where Amoy money wouldn't be accepted by the local peasants.

Q: Fragmentation of the...

Adm. M.: Yes. Also the Amoy language wasn't understood. They were just that fractionated. There was someone, and I've forgotten who, who explained that aspect of the history of China, and the tiny compartmentations of people, money, language, and so forth, all along the southeast coast. Well, here we were, we were all out there for three years or two and a half, more or less, whatever it turned out to be, and we were going to be in that country and we might as well have a good introduction to it like this, thought Captain Nimitz, upon which, thereafter, to build by our own devices our understanding of the country. Why not learn something about it if you're going to be here two and a half years? And that was just another little facet of his belief in the way things ought to be done.

Q: Let me ask you if the officers from other ships in the Asiatic Fleet were so benefitted?

Adm. M.: I never heard of it. I never heard of it. But the effects were profound among our people. It led people to do things like taking leave when the ship was in Shanghai, getting on the railway train and going up to Peking, and thence down to Chinwantao, on up to Harbin, where you could go by rail in Manchuria, and thence down through Korea, and come home by ship from Korea. These were the next steps into taking a look for yourself, and extending this fine introduction that he had provided us in this unparalleled way.

Q: Seizing your opportunity, using your time.

Adm. M.: Yes.

Q: Mrs. Lay told me that - I suppose the same principle prevailed in the family, insomuch that when she came out there to be with the family, she had to enroll in a course for secretaries or something of the sort to keep her out of mischief.

Adm. M.: It was a very close family, one would judge from a very remote outside position looking in, as far as family affairs were concerned. When all the ensigns would be sitting around the swimming pool at the Army and Navy Club in Manila, and here would come the captain, and there would be Mrs. Nimitz, there would be the little girl, and if he was going to play tennis, why, they might go swimming in the pool or something like that. They came together and they did things together.

Well, I suppose I've nearly run out of the anecdotes that always attract my memory the most strongly, unless you have some more questions.

Q: No, I think I've utilized what questions I had as you went along. The only other thing I can think of at the moment is this: in talking with people who knew the Admiral, I've attempted to make a collection of his well-known stories. The biographer is interested in this. Do you happen to remember any of them? He was a very famous raconteur, and...

Adm. M.: I'm afraid I don't. Obviously that's exactly what was going on at that dinner party in Newport that I spoke of at the Hamels' home, where people just stood around fascinated by his conversation, before and after dinner. I remember learning early in his time aboard the Augusta while we'd be, let's say, steaming in some quiet watch in the Pacific, that he had commanded one of those little gunboats that we operated in the Philippines right after we defeated the Spanish, while we were going through what was called the pacification. He used to talk about that often to me, because he knew that my father had also commanded one of those. And I have a considerable background of vague lore in my mind about the operations in those little gunboats, but I can't exactly sort it out, what I learned from Admiral Nimitz' tales or from other sources.

I know they were little things. The one my father commanded was called the Samar. It was an ex-Spanish gunboat, and I'm not sure in what condition the Spaniards surrendered her, whether they had scuttled her and we raised her and used her, or what. But you know the geography of the Philippines - 14,000 islands, or something like that. Anything we wanted to do all down through those islands meant a substantial investment in things that floated, in order to get the troops there, and to keep them fed while they were there, and to help them out. My father used to tell me tales when I was a little boy of his adventures with the Samar, and Captain Nimitz had many amusing stories from his days as a brand new officer. This was about 1899 or 1900, that my father had his. Obviously it was quite early in Admiral Nimitz' career that he would have had one.

Q: Yes, because he was the class of 1905.

Adm. M.: Yes. Must have been in his very first year or so. My father was the class of '96. He was on Admiral Sampson's staff off Cuba in 1898, and he went from there to the Philippines in '99, I think, and he had the Samar out there.

Well, Captain Nimitz knew that and of course he knew the Philippines. The Philippines were an area of great interest to everyone in the ship and, indeed, I suppose that brings up a few more things.

One of our regular tasks out there, which we'd do every winter, was to go all around through the Philippines, through obscure, out-of-the-way places that might conceivably serve as ports or shelters or something in wartime, and do a little looking around and check the accuracy of the charting as to the hydrographic features, what else was there, and what flat areas might be airfields, where could you have some defenses...

Q: Was this the foresight of Washington or of the Admiral or of the Captain?

Adm. M.: I think it was the foresight of the Commander-in-Chief of the Pacific Fleet, Admiral Upham. I'm not sure there, because I'm not sure to what extent the Houston had done that same thing. We certainly did it every year, spent a lot of time down in what we called the Southern Philippines. Go in all of these out-of-the-way places. Well, I mentioned one, Tutu Bay. For heavens sake, who ever heard of Tutu Bay?

Q: I've got to look that up.

Adm. M.: We were in there in the Augusta. All those places, many of which had never been visited by a modern U.S. man-of-war, and most of which had not been visited since pre-World War I days, and that sort of thing, and in we'd go. And, as usual, everything was done very thoroughly. Groups were all told off to go there and look into that, you go there and look into that, put it all together, and send it back to Washington, I suppose.

I have to tell you one more. We went down to Australia in 1934. This was for what was called by the Australians the Melbourne Centenary, being the 100-year anniversary of the founding of Melbourne or the State of New South Wales or whatever it was the anniversary of. Big celebration. England-to-Australia air race, coming in to Melbourne, and all of that.

We went down there, and some of the officers had been to Australia before, and they told us all kinds of wild tales about the fantastic levels of entertainment and so on. But we China Station ensigns sort of discounted all of this pretty heavily...

Q: You were a little blasé.-.

Adm.M.: Oh, yes - we could see through that smokescreen. Well, when we got there we found that it was all that they had said, and a great deal more. And, of course, incidentally, when I went down there in '56 with my destroyer squadron, I tried to tell my destroyer captains about this, and I got the same, you know - I could see the looks of disbelief on their faces. They found out the same thing.

Anyway, we wound up with in the wardroom of the Augusta, a big chart with every officer's name down, for every day, and each day was divided into four parts. And the days that officers had the duty, why, those spaces were blanked out, you see, but the days when you weren't on duty, your day was allocated to up to four different social invitations during the day. One in the forenoon, one in the early afternoon, and one in the late afternoon, and one for some evening function. Those were the four columns. And because there were so many of them, that you just had to do this in order to make sure that as many invitations as possible were acknowledged. Just sort of a little facet of the Nimitz organization.

Of course, those visits around through those Southern Philippine ports were old areas revisited, to him from his gunboat days, because that's where those gunboats went, through those places. Many of them were perfectly usable by the Augusta, adequate sizes, bays and so on, adequate depths of water, but completely remote. Go into one of those things and anchor the ship, and here'd be a beautiful bay almost completely landlocked, and we'd be looking at nothing but just dense jungle surrounding it. Fairly high ground rising. There were natives there. Sooner or later a few dugout canoes would appear and if you looked hard you'd see thatched huts through the trees. Very primitive, very remote, and the kinds of places that we made a lot of use of in World War II.

Mustin - 74

Q: I was going to ask, can you say that the spadework accomplished by the Augusta paid off in future years?

Adm. M.: I'm sure it did. You know, when I went from the Miami to Admiral Lee's staff and began, then, the continuing access to the most highly classified intelligence material and reports and so on, what our behind-the-lines forces were doing and our own guerrillas and our contacts with them, then I could recognize the pattern of the places we'd been. We were using these places. It was just too much for the Japanese to keep an effective surveillance over, and we just used them, you know, the road was never closed right into Manila for our people, our agents, in or out.

Q: Well, Admiral, you have been absolutely magnificent in your account of this whole period. I can't say how grateful I am to you for it. I think it truly adds something most significant to the records which the biographer will have to work with.

Adm. M.: I hope it will. I hope it will, because I think really there is one of the most magnificent figures that history will be able to identify, if history is ever able to do that. He really was a self-effacing sort of a person. I think he probably was far more of a man in every way, without any discredit to Eisenhower, than was Eisenhower. And yet the system picked out Eisenhower and touted him and made him President of the country. Nimitz shunned that, but in the same arena of trial and testing, which was World War II, I think Nimitz faced a hundred tough decisions for every one Eisenhower faced, with a fraction of the resources and infinitely greater peril, etc., etc., really.

When I read some of the earlier accounts, for example, of the tremendous decisions that Eisenhower had to make about do we or don't we launch the invasion, and when I think of what information was available to him, how much planning was behind this, what was known at that moment about everything bearing upon it, my tendency would be to say, well, for the love of Mike, this is no problem, this is a set piece, it's all ready to go, just say, go. And what in the world reason would you have for not saying, go?

That's a naval officer being a little critical, maybe, because it wasn't a set piece in the Pacific, ever, and you could lose your shirt. You were on the brink of catastrophic surprise constantly. Even in the later days when it had really become an American lake, when we could go in against the mainland of Japan and bombard those northern steel mills, for example, with battleship guns.

Since you've got that tape recorder going, let me tell you what happened. The first bombardment was a steel mill. Of course, there were piles of coal and tanks of oil, and all that stuff around it there, and we had carefully planned...

Q: This was on Kyushu?

Adm. M.: I've forgotten even where it was. It was the bombardment that Admiral Lee had planned and then had to turn over to the other fellow. The first thing we were going to do, we were going to start at one end of that complex, the downwind end, so that all the smoke and fire from all the things that you'd set on fire wouldn't blank it out, hide the rest of the things you wanted to hit. Second, we were going to use bombardment ammunition with reduced charges, because there was quite deep water there and we could get in range. The bombardment ammo had a shorter range even with full charges because the projectile was lighter and carried a lot more explosive, could do a lot more damage to that type of target than would the armor-piercing.

The first thing that happened was that this outfit that relieved Admiral Lee came in at the planned time in the morning, turned to the intended firing course with the ships that were to hit this target, and steamed down the line outside of gun range of the target. This clown who was the gunnery officer knew the maximum range of the guns with the kind of ammunition that had maximum range, but that wasn't the maximum range with the kind of ammunition prescribed for the event. So he steamed past the target once out of range.

Then, they turned around and they started back and, sure enough, the eager beavers start shooting at what looks like the biggest, fattest target first, and that one is upwind, and they set it on fire, and thereafter they never saw a single thing they were shooting at. They just dumped 'em in there by indirect fire and patterned them around a little, and hoped they'd accomplished the desired result. And I'll bet you that is not anywhere in the history books. But that's what happened.

Q: Interesting. Well, thank you so much, Sir. Thank you.

INDEX

for an interview

with

VICE ADMIRAL LLOYD M. MUSTIN, U. S. NAVY (RET.)

Adams, Charles Francis, 27-28

Amoy, 65, 67-68

Arnold, Julian, 66-67

Asiatic Station, 2

Atlanta, 6-8

Augusta, 1-5, 29, 36, 39-51, 56-57, 61-68, 70, 72-74;
 Inspections, 52-55

Australia, 72

Bremerton, 2

British, 10, 64-65

Burke, Arleigh A., 21-22, 24-25, 38-39

Canopus, 47-50, 53

Casco Bay, 25

China, 2-3, 40, 42-43, 64-68, 72

Dahlgren, Joe, 56-57

Draper, Charles Stark, 25

Eisenhower, President Dwight D., 74-75

Enterprise, 6

Gilberts Campaign, 8

Guadalcanal, 7

Guam, 9-10, 26, 30, 33-34, 36-37

Hamel, Roger, 28, 70

Hill, T. B., 36

Hong Kong, 65

Houston, 41, 65, 71

Hussey, George F., 38-39

Ingersoll, Royal E., 2

Isabel, 65

Iwo Jima, 31

Japan, Invasion of, 9, 30, 34-35; operations against, 12-14

Johnson, Nelson, 66

King, Admiral Ernest J., 9, 11, 18, 32, 34-35, 38

Lamson, 4-5

Lay, Mrs. James T. (Catherine Nimitz) 29, 69

Layton, Edwin T., 36

Lee, Fitzhugh, 36

Lee, Admiral Willis A., 8-11, 19, 21, 24-25, 30-35, 37-39, 74-76

Leyte Gulf, 10, 13, 31-32, 37

Manila, 41, 65, 69, 74

Marianas Campaign, 8, 12

Marines, 13

Marshalls, 8

Martell, Charles, 39

Mercer, Preston V., 35-36

Miami, 8, 30, 74

Midway, Battle of, 7

Mitscher, Admiral Marc Andrew, 21, 37

Murray, George, 6

Musashi, 17

Mustin, Mrs. Lloyd, 64

Naval Academy, 1, 42, 58, 64

Nimitz, Catherine (see Lay)

Nimitz, Mrs. Chester W., 69

Nimitz, Chester W., Jr., 62

North Carolina, 10, 29

Okinawa Campaign, 9, 30

Pearl Harbor, 7, 11

Philippines, 8, 56, 70-71, 73

Piedmont, 60

Richardson, James O., 2

Samar, 33

Samar, 70-71

Sampson, Admiral, 71

San Diego, 8

Shanghai, 65-68

South Dakota, 9-11, 30, 33

Thetis Bay, 26

Tirpitz, 10

Tonga Tabu, 10

Tsingtao, 43, 47-49, 64, 67

Tutu Bay, 55, 71

Upham, F. B., 41, 53, 71

Washington, 10, 29

Washington, D. C., 9-10, 14, 16-19, 25, 28, 32, 34-35, 38-40, 71-72

Waters, Admiral Odale D., 47

Whiting, F. E. M., 40

World War II: battles and campaigns, 7-9, 12-14, 20, 30; VT fuse, 14-17, 38; uniforms, 17-19; battleships, 29-30

Wyoming, 22

Yamato, 17

Yangtze River, 44

DECLARATION OF TRUST

The undersigned does hereby appoint and designate as his (her) Trustee herein, the Secretary-Treasurer and Publisher of the United States Naval Institute to perform and discharge the following duties, powers, and privileges in connection with the possession and use of a certain taped interview between the undersigned and the Oral History Department of the United States Naval Institute.

(1) As an <u>Open</u> transcript it may be read (or the tape audited) by qualified researchers upon presentation of proper credentials as determined by the Trustee. In the case of interviews about the late Fleet Admiral C. W. Nimitz, it is intended that first use of the material shall be made by the biographer of the Fleet Admiral, Professor E. B. Potter, and the Naval Institute is authorized to deal with the material in this fashion.

(2) It is expressly understood that in giving this authorization, I am in no way precluded from placing such restrictions as I may desire upon use of the interview at any time during my lifetime, nor does this authorization in any way affect my rights to the copyright of any literary expressions that may be contained in the interview.

Witness my hand and seal this 1st day of May 1970

[signature]

I hereby accept and consent to the foregoing Declaration of Trust and the powers therein conferred upon me as Trustee.

[signature]
Secretary-Treasurer and Publisher

Interview with Rear Admiral Odale D. Waters, Jr.

By John T. Mason, Jr.

Date: 14 July 1969 in Alexandria, Virginia

Q: Admiral, how good of you to give me a little of your time this afternoon to talk about the late Fleet Admiral Chester Nimitz. Mrs. Nimitz told me that you had an intimate relationship with him and that, undoubtedly, you could add something - something of great value - to the material I am collecting in preparation for a biography. So, would you start out, Sir, by telling me when you first met him, and we'll proceed from there?

Adm. W.: Well, it was really sort of a stroke of luck that we in the USS Augusta got to have Admiral Nimitz - then Captain Nimitz - as our commanding officer.

Q: What year was that, Sir?

Adm. W.: That was in 1933. I went to the Augusta in '32 and my first captain was Captain J. O. Richardson, who was a four-star admiral.

Q: Another illustrious gentleman.

Adm. W.: A very fine man. Then in the spring and summer of '33, we were ordered to leave the West Coast - we were home ported in San Pedro, at the time - to go to the China Station as the flagship of the Asiatic Fleet, and Admiral - then Captain - Richardson was relieved by then-Captain Ingersoll, who was also...

Q: Was that Royal?

Adm. W.: Royal Ingersoll. He was later on an admiral, and

he relieved, as I remember, in something like June of '33. It happened, I think, that he had some sort of a family problem - I believe it was his mother who was living with them who was very ill - and Admiral Nimitz, at that time Captain Nimitz, was ordered to the new cruiser Indianapolis. But because of Captain Ingersoll's problems, he and Captain Nimitz swapped commands along in the late summer or early fall. So that Captain Nimitz ended up taking us out to the China Station in October of '33, and I felt I was extremely fortunate as a junior officer to have been associated with three such people as...

Q: What was your duty on the Augusta?

Adm. W.: Well, I was a junior officer then and I started off being the F Division, the Fire Control Division, one of the JOs and eventually worked my way up to being the Division Officer before I left the ship. And it was a wonderful cruise. I think that all of us in the ship profited so much by being at such an early age under a man of Admiral Nimitz' personality and leadership. He was...

Q: In just what fashion did you benefit so greatly?

Adm. W.: Well, we learned by assimilation, I think, and particularly by example from a man of his type. For example, Captain Nimitz was a man of great force and, of course, of tremendous competence, but he was also a man who was always in control of himself, and I have never seen him openly angry at any time. I've seen him when I knew he was angry because you could tell that because his light blue eyes sort of flashed lightning. But he never lost the grip on himself where he balled anybody out in front of anybody. This always took place in the privacy of his cabin. It happened to me, it happened to other junior officers. But I think that the reason he was such a great leader - one of the reasons - is that he had tremendous self-discipline and he was always calm in any emergency. He never allowed himself the liberty of losing his temper, shouting, screaming the way some people do under duress, and this was a great lesson to all of us. And it was quite obvious in the ship that this sort of leadership had its effect because the Augusta under Captain Nimitz' command won the gunnery trophy that year, which was very hard to do because we were away from the rest of the Fleet. We won the Iron Man in athletics for cruisers. We were sort of tops in everything we did. We were right at the top. It was a tremendous ship and a great experience.

Q: Were you more or less prepared for Admiral Nimitz - Captain Nimitz, at that time - coming to the Augusta? Did you know something about his reputation before he was assigned to her?

Adm. W.: Only very slightly. Of course, he was a rather young man at that time. As I remember, he came from command of a submarine tender, I believe. His reputation did come before him, but he really hadn't made his mark at that time, but he soon did with us.

Q: He established it, right there.

Adm. W.: Yes, and the ship was a great ship. It was one of these ships that was well run, and everybody did his job and, at the same time, it was a happy ship.

Q: It was a happy ship.

Adm. W.: It was a happy ship because everyone was supporting the captain all the time and we just thoroughly enjoyed it. I've always looked back and thought of the tremendous advantage it was to all of us young officers to have had an experience like that.

Q: His son tells me that with him and with others - he knew it was true - that the Admiral didn't exactly tell you that he expected you to accomplish certain things, but it was kind of an unwritten thing, you knew instinctively that his standards were high and you'd better measure up. Was this the sort of thing that prevailed?

Adm. W.: That's exactly right. You sort of did it automatically. You did your very best for him because he was a fine man and a great seaman amongst other things, a great shiphandler, a great leader. When standing watch on the ship, you were always on your toes trying to do the job right. A junior officer is allowed to make a mistake and sometimes you don't do the job right. But we all tried.

Q: What was his method of correcting you when you made a mistake, Sir?

Adm. W.: Well...

Q: Give me an illustration.

Adm. W.: I can give you an illustration of that. He used to - he had a system what was, I think a very good one, of letting the younger officers handle the ship, and he kept a sort of a record, and you might be getting under way or coming to anchor and you'd hear your name passed over the loud-speaker system to report to the bridge, and he'd say, "Mr. so-and-so, take the ship and get her under way," or "take the ship and bring her to anchor." And I was bringing the ship to anchor one time, when it was my turn to do these things down in the southern Philippines, and I was trying my best to do a good job, but I came in too fast and I ended up backing the ship full power astern. I think, as I remember, I laid out something like 90 fathoms of chain, and finally got her stopped, with no word from the captain at all. He just stood there and watched, and when I got all through and then had to heave back in to, say, 60 fathoms to get the ship secure, he said, "Waters, you know what you did wrong, don't you?" And I said, "Yes, Sir, I certainly do. I came in too fast." And he said, "That's fine," and that was the end of it. That was the kind of a man he was. I think one of the things I've been thinking over that is a good example of how his leadership worked is that when he was relieved, and I think that was 1934 - 5, I guess - anyway, we were in Shanghai and we were tied up to buoys in the middle of the river opposite Yangtzepoo, where the cruisers always moored in those days, and Captain Nimitz was relieved by Captain Gygax, who also was later on an admiral, and he and his family were leaving on one of the Dollar liners, I think it was the <u>President Cleveland</u>, which was moored upstream from us, several berths away, and after all the change of command ceremony unbeknownst to Captain Nimitz, the junior officers secured his gig, his ordinary gig that he travaled in, and we manned one of the lifeboats - we had pulley lifeboats in those days, whale boats - we manned the boat in style, the way you were supposed to do in those days, we had frock coats, gold-striped trousers, epaulets, cocked hats, and we were at the foot of the gangway when the captain came down to go to the ship, and we rowed him up to his ship. He was quite delighted with this. The coxswain made him honorary coxswain and he took the tiller and we rowed him up to the landing float alongside the Dollar liner, and then he insisted that we secure the boat there and all come aboard and have a drink with him, which we did. When we got back to the ship the photographer took a picture of the boat crew, all in our finery, and I still have one of those pictures around some place. I remember it took a 12-man crew to row her and we had a coxswain, so that was 13 in all, and of those 13 officers, four of them became flag officers.

Q: That's the nearest one could come to royalty, isn't it?

Adm. W.: Well, I think it all goes back to Captain Nimitz. Of that group of junior officers a pretty large percentage, a much larger percentage than the average, became flag officers.

Q: That a wonderful attribute to give a man like that. When next did you associate with him?

Adm. W: Well, when he left the ship, he was going back to what was then the Bureau of Navigation, and he told all of us that when time came for us to be detached to write him our preference and he would see what he could do for us. He felt that he had a good ship and that he could reciprocate in some way by placing these young officers. So, of course, all of us did, we took him up on his fine invitation. Invitations like that are rather rare.

Q: Yes, I imagine so.

Adm. W.: He was Assistant Chief in the Bureau of Navigation, I think. So when the time came for us to be detached, all of us around my time - we were building new destroyers then and we wanted to go as part of a ship's company with the new destroyers - and so we all wrote to Captain Nimitz. Every one of us got a new destroyer assignment when we came home a year or so later from the China Station. So he really produced. He not only gave us an invitation, but he made good on it.

Q: That was characteristic of him, wasn't it? I mean keeping in touch with promising officers.

Adm. W.: Yes, it was. I didn't actually serve with him any more. I was never under his immediate command. I did, during the war, when I went to Pearl, of course, I stopped in and called on him, and anybody of the old crew of the _Augusta_ was always welcome, of course. But I never really served with him again directly, and my last contact with him was in - let's see, I came here in '65, it was either, I think it was February of '65, when I was Commander, Mine Force and Commander Naval Base at Los Angeles, and on the occasion of his birthday a lot of flag officers out there arranged to fly up to San Francisco and have lunch with Admiral Nimitz at his quarters on Treasure Island. And there was a rather large crowd of us there - I think the total number at lunch was something like 25.

Q: Was that No. 1 Yerba?

Adm. W.: Yes. We had a wonderful time. Of course, it was a stag luncheon and I felt a little bit quilty after it was over because I think I was the only old Augusta boy there, and the Admiral mentioned something about it and I started telling stories on the Admiral and he started telling stories on me, and we sort of monopolized the luncheon conversation. But it was a most pleasant time. Then, at the end of the lunch, Mrs. Nimitz came down in the gilded cage, the gilded cage, the elevator at the quarters, and we had a chance to speak with her. That was the last time I saw the Admiral. He was in great spirits, and, of course, he was a wonderful storyteller.

Q: Do you remember any of his stories? I've been making a collection of them.

Adm. W.: Not off hand. I hadn't thought of...

Q: They can be off-color, that doesn't make any difference. I know many of them were.

Adm. W.: No. I think you've kind of caught me short there. Because I was with him at various times, such as when I was working for Admiral Wright on the SacLant staff in the middle '50s, we had a flag mess there and on one occasion I remember Admiral Nimitz came through and he was at lunch, and that was a great day because he told story after story that day at lunch.

Q: He prided himself, apparently, on collecting these stories. I was trying to find out from Mrs. Nimitz whether he composed some of them himself. They were so numerous and

Admiral Waters - 9

so fabulous.

Adm. W.: It wasn't long after I left the Augusta and he was still in Washington, and Captain Billy's Whiz Bang - do you remember the old magazine Captain Billy's Whiz Bang, it was sort of the forerunner of, well, not Playboy, but it was a raffish type of magazine...

Q: Yes. Yes.

Adm. W.: ...and there was a cartoon in there with a sailor, who wore the old 13-button, flap-trousers, and all that, except he had them on backwards, and of course he had the flap in back and the Chief was saying to him, "I don't give a dam how many pills you've taken, put those pants on right," and Admiral Nimitz had this cut out and duplicated and sent it around to a lot of us, and he scribbled on it, "Would you know anything about this?" I've still got it framed at home some place. I've carried it around with me.

Q: You say that on the occasion of this birthday party on Treasure Island, you were able to tell the assembled multitude some stories about the Admiral. Tell me some of those stories.

Adm. W.: Oh, gee, that's pretty hard to do. It's pretty hard to think of things like that...

Q: Cast your mind back on the cruise itself and some of the circumstances, some of the incidents which were involved.

Adm. W.: Well, there was a - one of the ones which comes to mind was an incident of Captain Nimitz at Mast, holding Mast on the enlisted men. I had a third-class petty officer, third-class fire controlman in my division. The ship was in

Tsingato, and this young fellow was ashore on shore patrol, and he was caught by the Shore Patrol Officer in the upstairs apartment of a White Russian cabaret girl with part of his uniform removed. This boy's name was Woolley and I'll never forget it because we went to Mast and he was charged with being out of uniform and dereliction of duty while on shore patrol. And, as is the custom, if a man in your division is on report, of course, you go up to stand beside him at Mast while the captain hears his story. So this report was duly read and Captain Nimitz stood there and said, "Well, Woolley, what have you got to say for yourself?" And Woolley said, "Well, Captain, it was this way. I was on Shore Patrol there and I was walking down the street and I snagged my uniform and tore it. I know that when you're on Shore Patrol, you're supposed to be dressed completely in every way, and a snagged uniform is a very bad things for anybody on Shore Patrol to have. This young girl happened to be a friend of mine and she offered if I would come up to her room to sew up the snag in my uniform. So that was why I was there with my jumper off. She sewed it up and that was why I was there." Captain Nimitz could hardly keep from laughing, but you could see that he thought that this was such an ingenious and good story that he had to give the man credit for it, so he dismissed the case. I told that story, and he said yes, it was true. He didn't quite break into a smile when I asked if he thought that was a great story and the fellow ought to get credit for having that much ingenuity. From then on, that poor fellow had a tough time in the ship because whenever we'd go to general quarters down in the plotting room - I was the plotting room officer and Woolley was on one of the range-keepers, I think - somebody would always say, when we'd get down and man our stations, somebody would always pipe up and say, "Hey, Woolley, tell Mr. Waters, have you had any hemstitching done lately?"

Q: Yes, a tough row to hoe.

Adm. W.: Captain Nimitz' farewell party was one of the greatest events I've ever gone to. It was held in Shanghai and we took over a whole big club there, and had a dinner and a dance, and all kinds of speeches and awards for the Captain. It was a great party. Do you know Leland P. Lovette?

Q: No, I don't.

Adm. W.: Admiral Leland Lovette. He wrote Naval Customs, Traditions, and Usage.

Q: Yes, I've heard his name.

Adm. W.: He was a very gregarious man, a very fine talker. He was the master of ceremonies and did a great job - he always did a great job being master of ceremonies at a party like that. After the party, or after the dinner, we were standing on the dance floor and he was standing there - I think he was talking to Captain Nimitz - and I was standing by when his wife came up and she said, "Leon, I don't know what's gotten into you. The party was very nice, but all you did tonight was talk, talk, talk, talk." He said, "My dear, you seem to have missed the whole point of the meeting."

Of course, we all laughed at him because it was so true.

Q: Did the Captain produce any of his stories on that occasion?

Adm. W.: Not that I recall. I think he was pretty emotional at that send-off. I don't recall any stories produced.

Q: Admiral, how would you analyze his great leadership ability?

Adm. W.: Well, of course, he was an extremely intelligent man. He prepared himself, that is, he knew his profession. Getting back to the principles of leadership: first of all, you've got to know your job, and he certainly knew his. And then he knew how to execute his job, he knew how to accomplish his end by getting his people to follow him rather than driving him them ahead, and he always looked after his people. I think those are the three big points that you really have to adhere to. If you didn't convince the people that you're trying to lead that you're on their side and looking out for them, why, I think this is a tremendous step forward to any successful job of leadership. I think it goes back to - remember the book, <u>Mr. Roberts</u>?

Q: Oh, yes, indeed.

Adm. W.: Well that was made into a hilarious stage show and movie, but it had some pretty good writing in it, and one of the things I remember - Thomas Hagan wrote it, I think - [Heggen(?)] one of the things I remember that always impressed me about it was that in the book Hagan says - it says of Mr. Roberts, the hero, that Mr. Roberts was a great leader because he

Admiral Waters - 13

never had to look over his shoulder to see if he was being followed. I think the same thing could be said of Admiral Nimitz.

Q: That's an interesting comment about Admiral Nimitz.

Adm. W.: He just knew they were there, and they will be if you treat them the way he treated his people.

Q: He obviously - he himself said this - exercised great care in the selection of his staff.

Adm. W.: Yes, he did.

Q: He told me once about making a mental notebook of officers coming into Hawaii from the South Pacific and various places, and he would always succeed in talking with them at some length about the battle or what-have-you and at the same time he was sizing the man up if he'd never known him before for a future assignment.

Adm. W.: By his calmness and looking out for his people, I don't mean to imply that he pampered anybody. He could be very stern when he had to be.

Q: He'd have to be.

Adm. W.: When discipline is required, you have to be that way. He was, but it was in the same calm way he did everything else. It was done on the Augusta. There were officers on the ship who were detached and sent other places who didn't measure up. That's the way you have to operate to maintain these things.

Q: Well now, Sir, you had that one tour of duty with him on the Augusta and only one where you were so closely associated and yet you succeeded in establishing a personal relationship, didn't you?

Adm. W.: Yes. Not too close. Personal in several ways - Christmas cards and that sort of thing - and then seeing him at various times. Another thing that sort of made our relationship with the Nimitzes a little bit closer was the fact that Bill Leverton, who was a class ahead of me and also became an admiral, was Admiral Nimitz' flag lieutenant after the Admiral made rear admiral. Bill was not only a shipmate but he married my wife's first cousin, so we had a bit of a connection there. We used to at least hear of and see the Nimitzes a little bit more than we would ordinarily. Then, as I say, the *Augusta* was such a close-knit ship that whenever a few of them got together there'd usually be an *Augusta* reunion party some place. Of course, if the Admiral was around, he always went to those.

Q: Did he consider, as he looked back on his career, did he consider that *the* ship?

Adm. W.: Well, I doubt if anybody ever said, you know, this is *the* ship because - but I think he always looked back on it as a very happy and such a successful cruise for him, and he was very close to so many of the officers, and quite a few of them served with him again after that. It just happened that my career didn't quite go in that direction of being able to - being available - to serve with him. But several of the officers of the old *Augusta* did. He was a great athlete, you know.

Q: Yes, tell me about his prowess there and how did he

accomplish anything of that sort on board ship?

Adm. W.: Well, of course, it wasn't possible to do very much on board ship. We did have a - the <u>Augusta</u>, as ships go these days, wasn't too large, you know, she was one of the 10,000-ton treaty cruisers - we did have fish nets that we rigged up in the well deck alongside the catapults on either side. And then we partially deflated a volley ball and rigged the volley ball net on the center line of the ship, fore and aft, and played from side to side with these fish nets, hopefully keeping it from going over the side. We had some very rousing games at sea. That was probably one of our best forms of exercise. And, of course, at that time, we were in port a fair amount of the time. We would go out for training exercises for two or three weeks, but we were never far away from some port that we more or less called a base, such as in the wintertime we were in Manila a lot, or up at Olongapo working, and spring and fall we'd hit the China coast, Hong Kong and Shanghai. The summertime we always spent in Tsingtao and while we worked hard when we were at sea, we got a fair amount of time in port. That was when Captain Nimitz played - he played a great deal of tennis, and there were half a dozen or so that...

Q: Were partners?

Adm. W.: ...were partners on the tennis courts. I wasn't a very good tennis player. I didn't make the team...

Q: Did you have a try-out?

Adm. W.: I wasn't good enough to try. I was a golfer and still am, but Sam Moncure and Bill Leverton used to play with him. Incidentally, Sam was close to the Admiral. He was one of his tennis players. He's here in Alexandria.

Q: Fine, I'll get in touch with him, and I wrote Leverton the other day. He's in North Carolina, isn't he?

Adm. W.: Yes. He had a heart attack after he made admiral and retired and is living down at Whispering Pines, North Carolina.

Q: Yes, Mrs. Nimitz sent his address to me.

Adm. W.: Sam was a very close friend of Admiral Nimitz' and he's right here in Alexandria. He retired from the Navy and is Vice President of the United Virginia Bank right here on King Street.

Q: You were talking about the Admiral's prowess as an athlete, he had a reputation as a very strong swimmer. Did you experience any...?

Adm. W.: Yes, we used to do a lot of swimming at Tsingtao and quite a few times in the open sea. We'd go out and if it was calm on a cruise we'd have swimming call. He also, as I remember, played soft ball with us. In Tsingtao we used to have a Sunday morning soft ball leaque where the married officers played the single officers. Every Sunday morning, we'd have it at the race track in Tsingtao, and he used to take part in those games. They were a lot of fun.

Q: And, of course, out in Hawaii, he was a great horse shoe player. He didn't do any of this, I don't suppose?

Adm. W.: He may have, at that time. I don't recall. I believe he did have a horse-shoe pitching stand at the house that he rented when we were in Tsingtao for the summer. And of course there was a beach there and he did a lot of swimming.

Q: Was his family there, at that time?

Adm. W.: Yes. Mrs. Nimitz and the children, the way most of the families did, followed us up and down the coast. They would always be in Manila when we went there in the wintertime and probably meet us in Tsingtao or maybe be in Shanghai when we stopped off on the way up. I guess most of them were. Then usually they would take a house for the summer.

Q: Well, you obviously experienced some of their hospitality?

Adm. W.: Oh, yes. Yes, indeed.

Q: Tell me about - try to re-create a scene at perhaps a dinner party or something.

Adm. W.: It's been so long. I can recall going to the Nimitz', you know, for a cocktail party or having some of the junior officers in for buffet. But I can't single out any single incident.

Q: Were you exposed to oak? That famous drink of his?

Adm. W.: Oh, Okolehao. Well, that's Hawaiian, you know. No, I don't think I was with Admiral Nimitz. Of course, it was before he took the ship when we had our longest stay in the Augusta in Honolulu, when I was on her, and that was the year before when Captain Richardson had the ship and we went out to the islands. We were in a Fleet program, sort of an annual Fleet exercise ~~program~~. A week in the islands and we performed Fleet exercises on the way back. That was my first introduction to okihao. I don't remember anything very significant, though. It tasted like all the other bootleg whisky.

Q: Mrs. Nimitz must have been a terrific help to him.

Adm. W.: Yes, she was. She sort of looked upon all junior officers as her boys, you know. She sort of took care of us. Looked after us. She's a great person. She had so many interests before she got arthritis, you know, and - well she still does a tremendous amount. She's had health problems, but at that time, of course, she was much younger and she was very much interested in painting. She did a lot of painting. We'd look over her shoulder and admire her work. She was very good.

Q: I gather from what the children have told me and what she said that it was a most interesting family life they had together, and a very close-knit one.

Adm. W.: Yes.

Q: And yet they all said that the Admiral's first loyalty was not family, but Navy.

Adm. W.: Yes. Well, I would say it was kind of a tie. But he never let the Navy down. He certainly worshipped his family and they were a very close-knit group. I don't recall young Chester at that time. He must have been at school some place. He may have been around part of the time, but

I don't recall him nearly as well as I do the younger girls, Catherine, and Nancy, and little Mary was about that tall. Cute little girl. She had - the youngest child I ever saw wearing glasses. She had a vision defect. Cute little thing anyway, then she had these little spectacles.

That was a great ship, great ship. We had a lot of fun with our British counterparts out there. The British had, of course, a cruiser flagship in their Asiatic Fleet at that time. And we always paired off with their flagship. Their flagship changed more often than we did. I remember pairing off with two or three, but I think the one that was there most of the time was the HMS <u>Kent</u>, one of the Country class cruisers. We had a lot of fun with them and when we were in Hong Kong they entertained us, and when we were in Manila we entertained them when they came down. Then when we met in Shanghai, we sort of had Dutch treat. There were lots of stories about those parties. We had a chaplain, at the time, a very well-disciplined man as far as his own indulgences were concerned. He didn't believe in drinking or anything like that. And, of course, the British had a Church of England padre who was delighted with parties.

Q: Somewhat different, yes.

Adm. W.: I remember our executive officer exchanging dispatches with the <u>Kent</u> trying to swap our chaplain for their chaplain. They turned us down, and then we had a party together in Shanghai and their chaplain, actually the poor man just had a slight accident coming in to the party, so he was not under the weather. He slipped on the stairs and fell and cut his head open, and he was taken to our Marine hospital, where they sewed him up and he was all right, but after that, they offered to trade even. We said, no, they had to throw in their number three turret because their chaplain was slightly damaged.

Q: Well, Sir, that's...

Adm. W.: I'm sorry I can't think of any of Admiral Nimitz' stories. When you leave I'll probably think of one of his famous stories, but if I do, I'll send it on to you.

Q: Yes, if you do...the Leverton story, but it's a Leverton version of a...

Adm. W.: It happened to the Leverton family.

Q: Oh, I see.

Adm. W.: This was, of course, after Bill Leverton had been flag lieutenant and Admiral Nimitz came to Washington - some years later - probably war time, and by that time the Levertons had - they had four daughters, just as we did, and they were pretty small, and Admiral Nimitz called up and wanted to speak to Helen Leverton. One of the children, one of the twins, answered the phone and he said, "Is your Mommy there?" She said, yes, and the Admiral said, "Well, can I speak to her?" and the child said, "No, because she's sitting on the pottie." He always thought that was just great and never stopped kidding Helen Leverton about it.

INDEX

for an interview

with

REAR ADMIRAL ODALE D. WATERS, JR., U. S. NAVY

Athletics and Exercise, 16-17

Aquinas, Sister Mary, 19

USS *Augusta*, 1-4, 7-11, 13-15, 17

Gygax, Captain Felix Xerxes, 5

Hagan, Thomas, 12

Indianapolis, 2

Ingersoll, Royal, 1-2

HMS *Kent*, 19-20
Lay, Catherine (Nimitz) 19
Leverton, Bill, 14-16, 20

Leverton, Helen, 20

Lovette, Leland P., 11

Moncure, Sam, 15-16

Navigation, Bureau of, 6-7

Nimitz, Mrs. Chester W., 8, 18

Nimitz, Chester W., Jr., 18

Nimitz, Catherine (see Lay)

Nimitz, Mary (see Aquinas)

Nimitz, Nancy, 19

President Cleveland, 5

Richardson, Captain J. O., 1, 17

Mr. Roberts, 12

Wright, Admiral Jerauld, 8

DECLARATION OF TRUST

The undersigned does hereby appoint and designate as his (her) Trustee herein, the Secretary-Treasurer and Publisher of the United States Naval Institute to perform and discharge the following duties, powers, and privileges in connection with the possession and use of a certain taped interview between the undersigned and the Oral History Department of the United States Naval Institute.

(1) As an <u>Open</u> transcript it may be read (or the tape audited) by qualified researchers upon presentation of proper credentials as determined by the Trustee. In the case of interviews about the late Fleet Admiral C. W. Nimitz, it is intended that first use of the material shall be made by the biographer of the Fleet Admiral, Professor E. B. Potter, and the Naval Institute is authorized to deal with the material in this fashion.

(2) It is expressly understood that in giving this authorization, I am in no way precluded from placing such restrictions as I may desire upon use of the interview at any time during my lifetime, nor does this authorization in any way affect my rights to the copyright of any literary expressions that may be contained in the interview.

Witness my hand and seal this 8 day of May 1970

Francis E. M. Whiting

I hereby accept and consent to the foregoing Declaration of Trust and the powers therein conferred upon me as Trustee.

R. E. Bowker
Secretary-Treasurer and Publisher

Interview with Vice Admiral F.E.M. Whiting   by John T. Mason, Jr.

New York City

Subject: Admiral Nimitz   Sept. 19, 1969

Mr. Mason: Admiral Whiting it's so very kind of you to assist us with this project. As you know, we are gathering this material for the use of the biographer of Admiral Nimitz. We're trying to reach as many of his friends, and the officers who knew him in a personal way, as is possible. And you certainly knew him in a most intimate fashion.

Would you begin, sir, by telling me when you first met him? Tell me about that, your first meeting with the Admiral.

Admiral Whiting: Thank you very much, Mr. Mason. I'm very pleased to be of any assistance to you that I can.

My first meeting with Admiral Nimitz was when he was in command of the AUGUSTA, at the Puget Island Navy Yard in October of 1933.

Q: When he first took over from Captain Ingersoll.

Whiting: Yes, I think Ingersoll had been the previous Captain.

We were outfiting to go to the Asiatic station at that time. I had been on the train for three or four days coming from New York to Seattle. I got aboard ship about noon and met the Captain; and started to unpack. About 3:30 that afternoon, I got a message from him - he'd like to play some tennis. He was quite a tennis fan, and so was I.

Q: Did he know of your prowess in this area?

Whiting: That I don't know, but I brought a couple of tennis rackets with me, and he may have seen them when I came aboard. I said, I'd be delighted to. He was in perfect physical condition, and I was a little worn out from the trip across the continent.

In the Puget Island Navy Yard, there were steps going up to a plateau. About 150 steps, and he took them two at a time. I came along puffing and grunting, thoroughly exhausted by the time I got up there. So, we had a good couple of sets of tennis.

Q: You were at a great disadvantage.

Whiting: Oh, well, that was part of the game.

I was, at that time, first Lieutenant of the ship. Later on, fleeted up to be Executive Officer, about 18 months during his tour.

Q: Had you known about Captain Nimitz's reputation prior to that meeting?

Whiting: I knew Captain Nimitz only in heresay. To go back prior to World War I; he had been ordered to Germany to convert diesel engines in Germany, the measurements from centimeters to inches. Later on, he superintended the construction of the engines in the New York Navy Yard. This goes way back to 1916.

He was Chief Engineer and Executive Officer of the MAUMEE, which was the first diesel tanker, she was an oil tanker in the Navy at that time. She had trouble cracking one cylinder from time to time. He kept her operating. After war was declared, she was assigned to half way across the Atlantic as a fueling station for destroyers that were going over there.

As a younger officer, and in connection with Admiral Rogers, who was in command of the TRAIN at the time; I naturally knew about Captain Nimitz. We followed the refueling of these destroyers with the greatest of interest. But, I had never had the pleasure of meeting him before I reported for duty aboard the AUGUSTA in '33.

Somehow or other, I never knew how, he had accumulated aboard the finest bunch of youngsters I had ever had the pleasure of serving with. They were a very lively crowd, and knew what they were supposed to do and did it. A good number of them went pretty near the top in the Navy during the World War. II

Whiting - 4

Q: Most of them were just out of the Academy?

Whiting: Lots of these youngsters were newly caught Ensigns.

Q: And they were all single men?

Whiting: No, Lloyd Mustin was married to Emily and they had a baby. I think he'd been out of the Naval Academy one year. Emily Mustin was one of the Howard clan, who was very famous at the Naval Academy during that period of time.

We had a very pleasant cruise, during his stewardship. Or during his command, is a better word to use. We circumnavigated Australia during the centennial which was quite a series of parties before we got through.

Q: This was the centennial of the establishment of the colony?

Whiting: Australia, yes. The Duke of Gloucester was there. We usually secured alongside the dock, particularly at Melbourne. There was an Australian cruiser on the other side, a British cruiser astern of her. In the morning you could always find most of our officers on board their ships exchanging the courtesies of the day. And most of their officers on the AUGUSTA drinking our coffee, which was the best coffee.

Of course, our boys were not drinking coffee on board their ships.

Q: No, they were drinking things which weren't permitted on ours. That was just showing the flag courtesy.

Whiting: That was all purely just showing the flag.

Q: That was a diplomatic venture. You, as the Exec, accompanied the Captain very often to the receptions?

Whiting: Sometimes I would, yes, of course. A good many times I stayed aboard ship and kept the ship while he was away. For instance -- he and the Admiral went up to Canberra. They were gone for several days. I, naturally, stayed aboard ship.

Q: Canberra was very young as a city.

Whiting: Canberra was half way between Sydney and Melbourne. They couldn't decide where to put the capital, as the story went. So, they put it half way between the two cities. It was practically a frontier town at that stage.

Q: It was still in the state of construction, wasn't it?

Whiting: Yes, it was still in the state of construction.

I think that they didn't have the proper quarters for the Admiral and the Captain up there, but I can't tell you too much about that because I don't know.

Q: Who was this, Admiral Upham?

Whiting: Upham, yes. He was there the whole time that Nimitz was.

Q: Do you recall any one of these diplomatic functions that you did attend with Captain Nimitz?

Whiting: No, none stood out. They were all official parties. Once the Captain and I got in a little trouble with Admiral Upham, I'm afriad. Both of us liked him a great deal. At Melbourne, we'd been at sea about a week or ten days getting there. We were asked as soon as we got there, if we'd like to play some tennis. Both the Captain and I said we'd love to. So, we dressed and went to the grass courts, which are beautiful in Melbourne. They set up a court for us, and four of us had some kind of a match.

We were a little late getting back to attend a reception which I think the Admiral and the Consul General were giving. We were frowned on a little bit, but he got over it before the afternoon was over.

Q: Since you mentioned the Admiral and tennis a couple of times, tell me about his prowess as a tennis player.

Whiting: Oh, he was a   man for his age, he was an excellent tennis player. He'd play with the youngsters, or take anybody on.

Tennis is a game you can play all over the world, and it was very fine.

My daughter was born out in Manila, and Mary had just outgrown her cot. So, Mrs. Nimitz turned the cot over to Mrs. Whiting. They were continuously doing little things like that that made the whole spirit of the ship one of high morale. We never had any disciplinary action that we had to take because of some misadventure. The morale of the whole ship was extremely high.

He had a straw hat that he used to wear, I don't know whether it had come out of Noah's Ark or not, but it was an antique.

Q: Panama type, with a broad brim, I suppose.

Whiting: He used to wear it. When he left the ship, when he was detached; the Ensigns were all going to row him ashore.

Whiting - 8

Their whaleboat was lying off. He took his hat and threw it over the side of the ship, and the Chinese coolies tried to get it. The Ensigns delayed his departure a few minutes while they recovered his hat, because they had great pride in it and they weren't going to let the Chinese coolies have it.

You remember those little incidents, and you don't remember some of the others. Another interesting thing -- We went up to Togo's funeral. He, of course, was the greatest hero in Japan. It was the most dignified ceremony that I have ever attended. We had about 50 or 60 Bluejackets in the parade, which lasted some time. We made sure that everyone of them was at least six feet tall.

Q: To lord it over the Japs?

Whiting: In a round about way to impress the Japs.

The next time that I served with him, was when he was Chief of the Bureau of Personnel. That was in 1940. I was ordered as Director of Recruiting, and he was the Chief.

Q: Had you kept in correspondence with him?

Whiting: We'd seen each other. He was in command of some experimental work out in the west coast, and I had a division of destroyers out there. We'd see each other now and then.

I regret to say, there was no correspondence, between us or anything like that. We would see each other from time to time.

Of course, he was Chief of Bureau of Personnel on December 7th. At about 3:30 in the afternoon, he'd come over from the Secretary's office to Arlington where our headquarters were. I went in to see him. He said to me, "Red, we have suffered a terrible defeat. I do not know whether we can ever recover from it." Looking back on it, ten days later he was out there, recovering as fast as he could.

Q: Tell me more about his attitude, as he imparted this news to you.

Whiting: He was most serious, and in an emotional state. So, were we all of course. I wasn't in the same echelon, by any means, with him; so he knew the story as best it was known; from the Secretary. He'd been there practically ever since we'd heard about this.

I first heard about December 7th, I was listening to a football game, when it broke in. Of course, we dropped everything and went right to the Navy Department. Our part of the Navy Department was over in Arlington. The main part of the Navy Department, and the Secretary's office, and the Chief of Naval Operations were over on Constitution Avenue.

I put the war plans in, recruiting, and so forth. I was on the telephone before three o'clock. I was told that in New York there was a line forming between Church Street and City Hall of men trying to volunteer.

Q: Here in New York?

Whiting: Here in New York. The same thing was going on all over the country. I went to report that to him, and what I had done. That's when he said, that we'd suffered a terrible defeat. And he didn't know whether we could ever recover from it. He was a very very serious-minded man when he said that.

Q: Did you see him again before he got out to Pearl?

Whiting: I saw him every day. He was very quickly on his way out there, and turned over his command.

Q: In the light of his remark on Pearl Harbor day, and the fact that he was naturally somewhat optimistic MAN, did you notice, almost immediately, a change to let's get with it, and so on?

Whiting: Oh, no. I don't know how soon he was told that he was going to relieve Kimmel. I do know that he was on his way very quickly.

Q: My intention was to ask if his attitude changed to an aggressive one, let's look forward and let's do something; before he left for Pearl?

Whiting: I didn't see very much of him after that one conference, alone. I didn't see very much of him, except to report every day that we'd taken in so many thousand men. And about the recruiting situation, which had not been very good, although we'd been able to meet our quota. We always seemed to be ahead at the starting point, but at the end of three months were always trying to catch up. After December 7th, we had no more difficulty with recruiting. I personally saw very little of him. He was too busy with whatever he was doing. I wasn't one to ask any questions.

That was the last I saw of him, until I went through Honolulu to take command of a cruiser division.

Q: When was this?

Whiting: That was 1944. Meantime, I had commanded the MASSACHUSETTS at Casablanca, and the Southeast Pacific. I did one little trip one winter when we were up in the Aleutians.

Our paths hadn't crossed, until I went out west to take command of Cruiser Division 14. That was right after the Saipan engagement.

He had moved out to Guam, during most of those later

campaigns, and of Leyte Gulf. I never saw him, until after the Okinawa campaign. My division was re-fueling in Ulithi, and I was detached with orders to report to him in Guam.

He said, "The Joint Chiefs of Staff have just decided that the Navy shall have command of Saipan, instead of the Army. I want you to get up there right away, and hoist your flag." I said, I had no staff, except a flag Lieutenant and so forth. He said, he didn't care, he just wanted me to go up there and hoist my flag. He wanted to make sure that we got command of it before the Joint Chiefs of Staff might change their minds.

Q: He was not a man to think in terms of large staffs anyway, was he?

Whiting: No. We had almost 100,000 troops on Saipan; and as island commander you had to have a fairly good administrative staff, and air personnel. The B-29s were operating out of there. I think the biggest flight they made from Saipan was 202. I'm not sure of that figure, but it was in that neighborhood. There was a lot going on, and we got a staff fast enough. Picked them up here and there from operations that were on the way out.

That night, before I left to go up to Saipan, he very kindly asked me to dinner. McMorris was there, and I think Flunkey.

Q: He's over in Portugal now.

Whiting: He had his doctor.

Q: Dr. Anderson.

Whiting: I've forgotten the name. The doctor, and McCormick. Wasn't McCormick his chief of staff?

Q: Yes.

Whiting: We sat around the table after dinner, and had the usual wardroom argument.

Q: That being?

Whiting: Wait, I'll finish this up. As many arguments do, this one resulted in a bet. I bet him $10 that the war would not be over that year. We would probably have to go through the Kyushu operations. So, he accepted the bet. Of course, the war was over in August of that year. I sent him a check for $10 immediately.

When he passed through Saipan on the way to Tokyo, as he got off his plane, I met him. He handed me a package which was a bottle of Johnny Walker Black Label, unheard of out there, in those days. So, I got a very cheap bottle of whiskey.

He was detached before I had a chance to see him again. I went up to Marcus to take the surrender there. He, naturally was up in Tokyo.

He was a great leader, and it was always a pleasure to serve with him.

Q: Reverting back to the AUGUSTA days, tell me about his manner of commanding a ship, and his concern for the training of the youngsters, and so forth.

Whiting: We had a fairly full complement out there. We were on our own, and the complement was permanent, relatively speaking. We went out there on a two or three year tour of duty, and we stayed out there on that one ship. A few people were transferred to smaller commands, and things like that. On the whole, you kept this crew permanently. That made life very simple and easy for everybody because you didn't have to worry about replacing this man and that man as you did when you served in the Atlantic fleet and the Pacific fleet.

There was no trouble about training. We knew what we were up against in the line of target practice and gunnery exercises and engineering things. As each step came along, you prepared for it and outlined what you were going to do, and went ahead and did it.

He was always extremely easy to work with. He was informal, yet you never took any liberties with him because there was no question that he was in absolute command of the ship. That was all there was to it. It was extremely pleasant, and I think one of the happiest cruises I ever had. Everything went so easily, we didn't have any trouble. Probably some of the others will say, it did. From my point of view, we had very little trouble.

Q: His family was out in China, was it not?

Whiting: Some of his family were. Mrs. Nimitz was there, and I know Mary was there. She was the littliest one.

Q: Nancy was there too.

Whiting: Nancy was. His son was not there, he was in school. I don't know if the older two girls were present or not.

Q: I know Nancy was. I think Catherine was there, too.

Whiting: From time to time, I think. This has been over 30 years ago, and I've forgotten.

Q: Mrs. Nimitz did a great deal about entertaining.

Whiting: Naturally, she was the Captain's wife. She came to dinner parties and receptions and things like that. Mrs. Upham was there, too, she was the Admiral's wife. Usually, she was on the ladies end of it.

Q: Was Mrs. Nimitz in Australia when you made the tour there?

Whiting: No, no wives were there in Australia.

We left Shanghai about the 4th of October. We went to Guam on the way down through the south Pacific, to Sydney, to Melbourne, to Batavia, to one other port. Where one of the young officers got into trouble because the Consul came aboard. When the Counsul left, the young officer fired eight guns instead of seven. The Admiral said, "Seven for the Consul and one for the pregnant wife." And the wife was pregnant.

During the war, I ran into the Consul again down in Chile. He remarked about the fact that he got eight guns, seven for the Consul and one for the pregnant wife, and she was pregnant. Then he introduced me to the son that had been born, 15 years before.

I came back to this country about the first of the year, January '46. Admiral Nimitz was then Chief of Naval Operations. I was only on duty in Washington for a couple of months before I came up here to New York in command of the naval base. After a few months here, I retired, to take civilian employment.

Our paths didn't cross, except when he expected to go to Pakistan, I believe in 1948 for the Kashmir situation. He was being briefed up here in the United Nations, which was a very young organization. Mrs. Whiting and I had dinner with him one night. That's the last I saw of him.

That's not very much --

Q: It's very interesting though. You started, when I interrupted you to revert back to the AUGUSTA, to more or less summarize Admiral Nimitz as an officer. Would you do that now?

Whiting: He was a leader, a great leader. Like all leaders, he was positive and knew his capabilities and was thoroughly competent in his instructions that he gave to people.

There's one little story that I forgot, you may have gotten this from other people. Once again, I have to go back twenty some odd years. My memory may be a little inaccurate.

Admiral Bruce Fraser, I think it was, had command of the small aircraft carrier out in China when Admiral Nimitz had the AUGUSTA. All of us knew each other.

At the beginning of the Okinawa campaign, there was a conference aboard one of the cruisers out there at which twenty or thirty Admirals attended. Admiral Nimitz flew down from Guam to Ulithi to tell us what it was all about. He said, "For the first time in this campaign we have our friends the British with us. they will be on the left flank, and if they need help and we send ships to them; those ships will operate under Admiral Fraser's command. And visa versa. If we need help, and he sends his vessels over to us; they will operate under our operational command." Then he kind of paused for a minute and then said, "Admiral Fraser and I had a long conference in Honolulu before this campaign was decided upon. He felt that he could operate for eight days a month, and we compromised on twenty." Then, without hesitating, he went on to some other subject.

Q: He compromised on twenty.

Whiting: It may have been twenty-two, but he called it twenty. It was a little breath taking.

Q: Does this indicate, in a sense, ---

Whiting: The British didn't stay up there twenty days.

Q: - the difference in an American point of view.

Whiting: I think that one of the greatest accomplishments that he achieved was the fact that we'd start out these campaigns with four groups. Let's say three carriers to a group. You would get to whereever you were going, you'd operate for three days, and then at darkness you'd retire. [ABOUT 200 miles] In the morning, there would be the necessary number of tankers. If you wanted ammunition, there was an ammunition ship. If you wanted a postage stamp, there was a postage stamp somewhere. As a matter of fact, we didn't need postage stamps; but that shows the completeness of the operation.

That train was always there, and you got whatever you needed, within limits. That train operated as long as the operation was in existance. In the case of Okinawa, I think it was almost two months. The Leyte Gulf operation was a long operation, too.

That was what enabled us to stay out there on the firing line, day after day after day, until the job was done. Nimitz deserves the credit, he had able people doing the work for him. The organization of that force which was operating, I don't know how many thousand miles from Honolulu, was one of the greatest feats in the war; I think. I always did think so.

Q: The completeness of it.

Whiting: Completeness, yes. He, as I said, had a fine service of supply; but he was the man who was responsible for it and the man, who through his assistants, got it going.

Q: That supply served a two-fold purpose, did it not? The actual ordnance needs, naval aspect; and also the human needs.

Whiting: What do you mean by the human needs? We had all the food, and everything like that that we needed.

Q: You said postage stamps, as a symbol. The point I'm trying to determine was - Admiral Nimitz was always noted for his understanding of people and his understanding of their needs as people. He also took this into consideration apparently when he was planning.

Whiting: That was the only way that we could have stayed out there. Without these supply ships --- bear in mind that they had to be coming out there all the time because we were gradually emptying those ships.

This group that I was in was the first group back. From Okinawa, for instance, we'd been up there for 48 days.

Out of the three other groups, some of them were up there 70 or 80 days. They couldn't have stayed there, unless every third or fourth day they could get replenishments because they used up an awful lot of oil and a lot of gasoline; and you had to eat.

Q: They used up energy too.

Whiting: That would be a day of rest, and we'd have a target practice if they wanted to, shooting drones, and things like that. On the whole, it was a day of rest because you knew you weren't going to be under attack.

Q: Then an island like Ulithi was set up for amusement purposes and recreation.

Whiting: The island of Ulithi was a beautiful harbor in the first place. There was a small amount of recreation. We'd get quite a lot of the crew and everybody ashore and we'd have beer in the junior officer's club and things like that. That was the recreation.

Q: Enough to break the monotony of being at sea.

Whiting: Broke the monotony, yes.

This has nothing to do with Nimitz, but I'll never forget as I was going back to the ship one night -- It was just before dark, we all had to be back by dark. There was a little Ensign there, I don't think he was 20 years of age. He kept saying, "I'm an ace, I'm an ace." He started to take off his clothes, and so forth. A shore patrol man stepped up and I thought there was going to be trouble. The shore patrol man settled it very quickly. He said, "And wouldn't your mother be proud of you now?" in a loud voice. With that, the kid got dressed and went back to his ship.

That shore patrol officer was an ex-policeman in New York, or something like that. He knew how to handle it, and he did perfectly.

Q: Admiral you spoke of this fleet supply train in being there in the middle of the Pacific. Was this a new concept?

Whiting: Oh, yes. We couldn't have operated and stayed out on the job as long as we did without it. In the Casablanca operation, we had one tanker there. We were always worried about oil.

This concept - there were three or four oilers, an ammunition ship, a cargo ship; a group of eight or ten ships out there. Of course, they changed as they became empty. The fact that they were always there, ready to meet the needs of the combatant ships made it possible for us to operate and change our HATS from 38 to 58. If the same ships were there, we'd just call ourselves by a new name.

Q: Admiral, isn't this in part an explanation? The fact that the U. S. Navy had this in the Pacific, and the British didn't have it.

Whiting: No, the British operated from shore.

Q: Isn't this an explanation in part of Admiral Frasers's remark that he could operate for eight days out of the month? Because he had to think in terms of supplies from shore.

Whiting: I suppose so. At the time, we'd gotten so accustomed to operating this way that we thought nothing of it until the operation was finished. Then we'd go back for a week. Halsey would take his whole staff back to Honolulu to get ready for his next operation. Then Spruance would bring his staff and take over, AFTER a reasonable amount of rest and recreation as you say. Then we went to sea again.

Q: And you, with your knowledge of the operations out there attribute this whole system --

Whiting: Nimitz in command of it, he engineered it as long as he got good people under him. He'd borrow somebody from the Standard Oil, or somebody like that, to run his oil, who knew oil. He'd borrow probably some from Armour's, and put him in charge of getting the meat out there. He was in command of it, it was his operation.

Q: I don't want you to think I'm laboring the point, but it seems to me that this is something that the biographer might well focus on.

Whiting: Yes, of course. Somebody who was intimately connected with that, could probably tell you a good deal more than I can. I was at the receiving end, and very glad to get what I could from him. And so was everybody else in 38 - 58. It was the thing that made the advance of this very large fleet. There'd never been anything like it, when you can stop to analyze it.

I made a little talk here after the war about it. I said, it extended from the Battery to Poughkeepsie. That kind of took their breath away; it was about sixty miles. Nimitz had these four groups, each of which had 20,000 yards to operate in. Maybe a little more than that. That's 80,000 yards or 40 miles; so about from here to Poughkeepsie. That was the size of that fleet.

Nothing like it ever before, or since. I don't suppose there ever will be, not in my life time.

Q: You said earlier that you have been involved in the Aleutian campaign as well. Was this with Admiral Kinkaid?

Whiting: No, I was up there later.

Q: Did you also have a similar, on a small scale, supply train there?

Whiting: Oh, yes. Some of the Alaskan people, and liberty ships would come up. We only lost one by submarine, I think, the whole time we were up there. At that stage of the game, they were developing one island in the Aleutians.

Q: Attu?

Whiting: No, it wasn't Attu. It was on Shemya. They had no harbor and it was very difficult to operate; with the idea that they might use it as a base for the B-29s flying to Tokyo. But it was just a little bit outside of their range. Also, the weather was terrible. We'd get snowed in for a week, and there was nothing you could do about it. Then it would clear for a couple of days, and then snow again for a few days.

INDEX

for an interview

with

VICE ADMIRAL FRANCIS E. WHITING, U. S. NAVY (RET.)

Massachusetts, 11

Maumee, 3

McCormick, Admiral Lynn, 13

McMorris, Admiral Charles H., 12

Melbourne, 4-6, 16

Mustin, Admiral and Mrs. Lloyd M., 4

Naval Academy, 4

New York Navy Yard, 3

Nimitz, Mrs. Chester W., 7, 15-16

Nimitz, Catherine (see Lay)

Nimitz, Mary (see Aquinas)

Nimitz, Nancy, 15

Okinawa campaign, 12, 17, 19-20

Pakistan, 16

Pearl Harbor Day, 9-11

Puget Island Navy Yard, 1-2

Rogers, Admiral, 3

Saipan engagement, 11-13

Shanghai, 16

Shemya, 25

Spruance, Admiral Raymond Ames, 23

Sydney, 5, 16

Tennis, 2, 6-7

Togo, Admiral, 8   Heihachiro

Ulithi, 12, 18, 21

www.ingramcontent.com/pod-product-compliance
Lightning Source LLC
Chambersburg PA
CBHW080616170426
43209CB00007B/1442